El Sid

El Sid

Saint Vicious

DAVID DALTON

ST. MARTIN'S GRIFFIN ≈ NEW YORK

Design by Bryanna Millis

Library of Congress Cataloging-in-Publication Data

Dalton, David.
    El Sid : Saint Vicious / by David Dalton.—1st ed.
        p.   cm.
    ISBN 0-312-18713-0
    1. Vicious, Sid.   2. Rock musicians—England—Biography.
3. Sex Pistols (Musical group)   4. Punk rock music—England—
History and criticism.   I. Title.
ML420.V365D35   1997
782.42166'092—dc21
    [B]   97-2876
                                                           CIP   MN

First St Martin's Griffin Edition: July 1998

10   9   8   7   6   5   4   3   2   1

CONTENTS

CONTENTS

ACKNOWLEDGMENTS

May all the *calaveras* of Oaxaca grow green hair and dance the pogo for *el hombre* clairvoyant and reckless, Jim Fitzgerald of St. Martin's Press, who aided and abetted this rant and its Sidspeak channelings and sent them out into the world.

On jungle-shrouded temples may monkey grammarians furiously scribble the name of Coco Pekelis who saved these scrolls from occult babble and befogged railing with her canny pentimenti and ruthless out-striking.

Let straight 8s thrum and barre chords hum for Lenny Kaye. Thanks for the muso chops and the gospel according to the Church of Punkitude, dude.

And, Susann, ta for the green 'air, darlin!

Before the explorers of Ground Zero of Punkitude, I abase myself. To Jon Savage for letting me use transcripts of his interviews with Sid's mum, the late Anne Beverley, and for making a copy of the out-of-print *Sid's Way* for me. And to Roberta Bailey for allowing me to use passages from her phone conversation with Sid.

I am also in the debt of the many murmurous evangelists, scribes, archivists, and exegetes of Punk, a short opinionated bibliography of whom follows:

England's Dreaming: Anarchy, Sex Pistols, Punk Rock and Beyond, Jon Savage. St Martin's Press, 1991.

This is the *Peloponnesian War* of punk histories, of rock histories in general, actually. Clearly the best rock history written to date. And I'm not just saying that because of all the stuff I nicked from 'im. Positively Medieval, it is, includin' such sundry matters as hoarding graffiti, housing, *louche* fashion, anarchist politics, social conditions (rotten, as ever), teen angst, history as camp, personal involvement (ya bloody wanker!), and the very thrust and urge of rock theology itself. Aw*right!*

Rotten: No Irish, No Blacks, No Dogs, John Lydon with Keith and Kent Zimmerman. St. Martin's Press, 1994.

Here he is, the most articulate, metaphysical and implacable rocker ever (in all 'is dandified fury). His characteristic mode of unrelenting abuse and contempt is offset by lyrical reminiscences of the era by his mates John Gray, Steve Severin, Paul Cook, Marco Pirroni, et al. (and his dad). Lovely touch, mate. Up to and includin' the ones I have meself written—wif rockstar molls and *soi-disant* hippie managers—this is me favorite rock autobiography. And don't fink you 'ave ta say somefin nice in return, ya tosser, the usual abuse would be fine.

The Sex Pistols: the Inside Story, Fred and Judy Vermoel. Omnibus Press, 1987.

The heady beginnings of Brit punk are bottled in this book. It's breathless, evangelistic, quaint, and scrappy the way these things tend to be at the appearance of a New bloody Jerusalem. The revised edition incorporates the diary of McLaren's secretary Sophie Richmond, with its wonderful juxtapositions of an upper-middle-class girl in a nest of seethin' yobs and overamped Svengalis, reading James Joyce on her lunch hour. Alas, in a postscript Fred succumbs to the dreaded Situationist fallacy.

12 Days on the Road: The Sex Pistols and America, Noel E. Monk and Jimmy Gutterman. Quill/William Morrow, 1990.

There's nothing like reading about mayhem and muckin abawt on tour, especially as recounted by a roadie. It's a little unfortunate that Noel (who went on to manage Van Halen) presents hisself here as the picture of long suffering reasonableness that he clearly wasn't. Hey, this is the bloody *road,* innit? Some fuckin' good stories embedded in the book, though. Should've been written in the first person.

Lipstick Traces: A Secret History of the Twentieth Century, Greil Marcus. Harvard University Press, 1989.

Sure, we'd all like to trace the great freight train of the European avant garde down to our favorite rock group. Don't get me wrong, I'm a huge fan of paranoiac-critical everything-is-connected grand unifying theories. And its all 'ere: Dada, radical politics, *insolite* epigrams, Matt Groening, mysteriographic texts, cultural history, Punk rock, kitsch, the Orioles, postcards, and the ever-fashionable Situationist heresy—pile it up! And, really, you can never read enough about Tristan Tzara and those wild lads wankin abawt in Zurich, can you?

So it was with some eagerness that I turned to the only substantial reference to Sid in the book to see where the mystic yob might fit into this cosmology. Imagine my chagrin, O my brothers, when I came to: "Sid Vicious, the crudest, cheesiest, stupidest member of the group." It was at this point I realized that as world-historical as the exigetic Greil may be, about some things he is clearly clueless. If you don't get Sid, mate, you don't get Punk.

Please Kill Me: the Uncensored, Oral Biography of Punk, Legs McNeil and Gillian McCain. Grove Press, 1996.

Wonderfully anecdotal and doomy. Oral history at its most sublime and grungy, right up there with *Edie*. The subtext of this book, of course, is self-justification and the rewriting of rock history. A revisionist work, in other words, that claims CBGBs Punk was the real thing and that Punk was purloined by a bunch publicity-manipulating limeys. In my opinion Legs should grow up and Danny Fields should stop whining. It's twenty bloody years ago, dudes. Nevertheless, a great fuckin read.

The Sex Pistols Diary: Sex Pistols Day by Day, Lee Wood; *The Sex Pistols File*, Ray Stevenson; *Chaos: the Sex Pistols*, Bob Gruen. All Omnibus Press.

Scrapbooks and books by photographers (Stevenson and Gruen). Some truly sweaty press clippings from the era, including hilarious and embarrassing commentaries by the various mums. And if you really need to know every show the

Sex Pistols ever played, *Diary* is a workmanlike piece of trainspotting.

Sid's Way, Anne Beverley. Virgin Books (out of print)
The Vicious family album. A book of baby pictures, snapshots, drawings, a radiant baby Sid, Sid going through various style changes. You see here the sweetness and goofiness of Sid, his various makeovers and refittings before he finally transformed himself into his demonic Other. A touching (almost wordless) scrapbook made all the more poignant by his mum's recent suicide.

And I Don't Want To Live This Life, Deborah Spungen. Villard Books, 1983.
This would be an astonishing book even if it weren't written by Nancy's mum. Nancy comes through in all her complicated glory, shattering our received images of her. A perplexed mother's tale, it is written with great compassion and unflinching honesty. It also contains some of the most hilarious Sid scenes ever. For anyone who's ever been a parent or a child.

And then, the *fons et origo* of Punk *écriture:* magazine articles. In the interests of brevity I'll mention only those by John Ingham (and the noble Savage) in *Sounds* and Charles M. Young's pieces in *Rolling Stone.* Better than any dispatches from the front you'll ever read because this was a war against a state of mind. Long may it flourish in all its tenaxed belligerence! Sod awf ya wallies!

Last but not least that creature of the zeitgeist, Richard Sassin.

READ THIS PAGE OR ELSE!
(a Roadmap to This 'Ere Book)

BLOODY STUPID QUES-
TION #1: *Is all that stuff in
BIG LETTERS and put in
BOXES (aka "Sid's Di-
aries"—see above) actually
writ by Sid Vicious?*

> **THIS 'ERE IS A EXAMPLE OF A PUR-
> PORTED DIARY ENTRY BY SID. SOD
> AWF, YA WANKERS!**

A course not, ya daft burke! It is by the alleged author
of this 'ere book.

VILE INTERROGOTORY #2: *Wot then is the source of this poxy
prose?*

As to how it come abawt is as follows:

One night while ponderin in me chamber waitin, waitin,
waitin for the Angel of Flight and Sleighbells to turn god back
on again and wot's this I hear then? A voice, I warrant, with
intent of great urgency speakin in the biblical or naval manner
of fings long past. With wicked comportment and salty wit
ee regaled me wif tales of yore when green 'air flourished
from Finsbury Park unto the East End. And takin' up me pen
I scribed it down all very faithful like in this book.

Now I willinly admit that I might well 'ave bin deceived
in this regard, to wit, that the above mentioned visitation might
'ave bin not of Sid but per chance of some naughty navvy with
a grievance against British Rail that I happened upon.

Notwifstandin', I believe wot I 'eard was of Sid 'isself
and 'ave written as such.

And, oi, Sid, if it weren't you, oo in bloody 'ell was it?

El Sid

1

Patient Zero

HE COULDN'T PLAY HIS INSTRUMENT, HE COULDN'T SING, HE was a mess. He was weedy, goofy, gullible, and psychopathic. Mindlessly violent. Sid was perfect. Even Elvis failed us in the end by becoming fat and pathetic, but not Sid. A nobody at seventeen, world famous at twenty, dead at twenty-one!

In the wake of such events there's always someone bemoaning the stupidity, the *waste* of these lives. Someone trying to make sense of it, someone admonishing us to *grow up*. When are you going to stop making these psychotic adolescents into tin gods? And then on the six o'clock news there's the rock critic trying to explain it while the smarmy anchorman feeds him his bromides: "Tell our viewers why a young man with fame, money, his whole life before him, would want to do this to himself."

But reason has no place here. We are in the Bat Cave, the liquid hydrogen is whining, the sibyl is shaking the bars of her cage, teenage boys are jerking off to a nude hologram of a nympho-maniac lizard woman. . . . And you, misguided soul, want to *explain* it?

> **I'VE GOT ABSOLUTELY NO INTEREST IN PLEASIN THE GENERAL PUBLIC AT ALL. I DON'T WANT TO BECAUSE I FINK THAT LARGELY THEY'RE SCUM AN THEY MAKE ME PHYSICALLY SICK, THE GENERAL PUBLIC. NINETY-NINE PERCENT OF THE SHIT YOU FIND IN THE STREET DON'T KNOW A FUCKIN FING. THEY ARE SCUM. AN I 'OPE YOU PRINT THAT.**

Go tell that teenager over there with green Tenaxed hair in a Sid and Nancy T-shirt that she is mindlessly buying into a maudlin cliché. That this so-called tragic hero is a worn-out scarecrow, a romantic banality invented two hundred years ago: the artist as outlaw, a pariah engaged in transgression, violence, and self-destruction in his quest to plumb being itself.

On the other hand who'd want to give stuff like this up? It's the very plasma of rock's phallic heart. No amount of common sense is going to make it go away. A discredited, vexatious delusion it may be, but by now it is endemic. Any child born after 1939 has this DNA imprinted in them—probably part of some failed government experiment.

So obsessed was Sid with the mythology of self-destruction that flagrant disregard for life and limb became routine. He ODed twice that year. He issued continuous bulletins about his eminent demise ("My basic nature is going to kill me in six months.") that turned out to be extremely prescient. The mythic Iggy was his idol. "I wanna be like Iggy Pop and die before I'm thirty," he told Roberta Bailey. When Bailey explained that James Osterberg was alive and well and living on the Lower East Side, Sid didn't buy it.

His taunting assessment of his friend John Lydon's fate—"You'll spend the rest of your life with people coming up to you and saying 'Weren't you Johnny Rotten once?' "— was not going to be his. Fuck no! His was the abbreviated timetable of a Rock Fable. A whole life from the age of eighteen 'til his death three years later flashed by in a fast-forward of streaked images. No rock star ever lived out a messier life.

When Sid sang "My Way" while shooting the audience he seemed to fulfill the ultimate teen fantasy. Yet Sid did almost nothing his way. As the creature of Punk subculture expectations, and a fervent devotee of various rock credos, he was constantly manipulated by others.

Johnny Rotten named him, Malcolm McLaren programmed him, Vivienne Westwood made his uniforms. He was fed a steady diet of poisonous ideas by his cynical handlers. Books on Charlie Manson, Nazi paraphernalia, murderous hatred toward the establishment.

He took speed, put on a Ramones album and taught himself to play bass *overnight*. Once given his new identity, Sid Vicious became a sort of golem to his own name, a malignant cartoon, a volatile human bomb. The toy that exploded.

Nihilistic spawn of the hippie reich, Sid became avenging angel and sacrificial victim for a shallow age of media-besotted fantasies—complete with his mum supplying the drugs that killed him and turning up with a $10,000 check from the *New York Post* for her "exclusive story."

Inextricably mediated and entwined with fiction, the Sid Vicious story has become as symbolic as that of any saint.

> AFTA ABOUT TWENTY MINUTES I JUMPED AWF THE DRUMS AND SAID, "THAT'LL DO, WE DON'T WANT TO ACTUALLY LEARN ANYFING, DO WE?"

A *vita* in which obnoxiousness, drugs, and psychosis came to epitomize England's overdue nervous breakdown. Sid personified the cyberpunk apocalypse, the last gasp of atom-bomb pop culture.

Like the Terminator, he seemed to have crawled out of future-rubble, the ruins of World War III. That's where he lived under the blown-up gasworks, circa 2014. To hell with the magnificent past of Imperial Britannia! Down with the glorious psychedelic revolution of Hippiedom!

2

Something's Wrong with My Baby

ROCK 'N' ROLL WAS NOW A SLATHERING BEHEMOTH IN AN Afghani jacket begging for change on St. Marks Place. The atom heart had stopped beating, its crass genius populi blubbering. What infamy! The most potent music in the world—Ibo war chants, Appalachian celtic keening—had fed into its bitches' brew like streams of liquid fire.

Rock supposedly had reached its pinnacle, its *ne plus ultra*, in the late sixties. But any clear-sighted yob could see this was deluded. The fuckin' *what?* Says *who?* Just at the point when those sixties farts thought rock had reached its high-water mark—had almost become Art—it was actually at the furthest point from its true nature, the original impulse, the First Ten Seconds. *Sgt. Pepper*, the prime exhibit in progressive rock, far from being its apotheosis, was clearly a betrayal, a kind of musical toadying to the establishment, an acceptance of conventional ideas of what music should be. It was prompted, if anything, by an innate contempt for rock.

Was it a good thing to have professors of musicology writing theses about you? No. Rock was about cocking a snook. It wasn't the *Mona Lisa*, it was Yoruba war masks, the snarling flash of the spirit calling into question established ideals of culture and sophistication, a barbaric yawp.

The pretentiousness of so-called "progressive" rock—what a fuckin' joke! The idea that rock had *matured* was nauseating. What could they be thinking of? They were serious wankers, those old sixties sods.

They were selling their patrimony for a mess of potage. Buying apartment buildings, pizza parlors. Eric Clapton poring over Three Dog Night's investment portfolios! The Rolling Stones, those primal rock dogs, buying canaries in Taiwan and condominiums in Boca Raton! The Who snapping up hotels and giving recently amortized pubs whimsical names!

3

The Cyberpunk

SID VICIOUS AND JOHNNY ROTTEN IN BERLIN, 1977. TWO MEN-
acing aliens from the same hellish planet. Gelled, spiky, bog-
brush hair. Gaunt triangular faces. Sunken eyes and zombie
gaze exuding leave-me-aloneness. Feral lizardboy delinquents from William Burroughs.

As the alpha wolves of the blank generation, they epit-
omized the psychotaxonomy of Punk: the no-future, no-exit,
end-of-everything look.

Adults kept blathering on about something called the
Second World War—an age of unspeakable horror and destruction. Hiroshima, Auschwitz, and the long, slow decline

and fall of the unholy British empire. Ancient history, ya wankers, so sod off!

Kids longed for anything; any catastrophe to relieve the boredom. *"Gimme World War Three so we can live again!"*

No empire, no future, no end, no god, no way out, and— far more horrible than any of these!—rock itself, dead at eighteen.

Rock 'n' roll, according to its own legend, had begun in a semi-mythological era in the ruminant American South (Elvis, Jerry Lee Lewis, Little Richard, Chuck Berry) and culminated in the acid rock of the late sixties (Hendrix, Dylan, the Rolling Stones). What else was there to say?

No one even referred to the youth culture anymore. There wasn't one. *"There is no future in England's dreaming.... No future! no future! no future! . . . for you!"*

4
Fast-forward

THE 1970S WOULD BE THE FIRST SELF-CONSCIOUSLY RECOMBI-nant age. Everything had been said, everything had been done. All you could do now was take pieces of the past and rearrange them.

As an alienated youth in London circa 1975, you were free to customize the future. With no credible sense of the past what else *could* you do? You gathered together whatever tatters of civilization you could lay your hands on. Bits and pieces of teen futurama lay in the cultural debris all around you: movies, science fiction, comic books, songs—especially songs.

Rock 'n' roll musicians sifted through obsolete styles as

if the past were a huge ruin from which they could scavenge the future. It was an intuitive perception having as much to do with TV's omnivorous eye as anything else (and you could always change the channel).

Anyway, the future was only a projection, right? Something that would take a particular shape if enough people believed in it. This was always the inner experience of rock 'n' roll. Adherents of the Noisy Faith said to themselves: See, there are all these layers of reality going on all the time. We're at, like, four removes from the cosmic drunk who's just understood the meaning of life, and about a dozen removes from the cold, phony, soulless, time-serving world of adults and business. What layer are *you* on?

> **"I AM A SEXLESS MONSTER TOTALLY BORED WIF THE WHOLE SUBJECT OF SCREWIN." PITIFUL TO REREAD ONE'S OLD PRESS CUTTINS. AT THAT TIME I DID FEEL LIKE A SEXLESS MONSTER ON ACCOUNT OF ME HEAD BEIN SHAVED AN WEARIN A VILE OLE TUXEDO THAT WAS FOUR SIZES TOO BIG AN ALL. I HAD NO MONEY WIF WHICH TO BUY CLOTHES AN PEOPLE WOULD RUN AWAY FROM ME WHEN I COME DOWN THE STREET. IT WAS A RIGHT LARF.**

Once adolescents established themselves as consumers (and then producers of their own fantasies) they set in motion an alternate reality, a second screen on which their movie could be played. The props: music, clothes, argot, sex, *attitude*. The annoying adult din of work and money and responsibility was simply tuned out.

From the minute the Teen Raj poked its pimply head above ground in the mid-1940s it began eroding the adult *reich*. For one thing, teens grow up. And while they don't bring all their teen fantasies with them into adult life, they bring as many as they can get away with. So the teen lifestyle, in turn, becomes part of the adult lifestyle. In the U.S.A. where "the pursuit of happiness" is part of the Constitution, it was only a matter of time before teen life became institutionalized and merchandized as a worldwide export. Everyone from Tehran to Singapore was soon hooked in to it in one way or another.

The teen worldview is one of danger, urgency, and menace. Children and adolescents are sensitive to crisis—their life is one impending disaster after another. The primal panic of the postwar years was the Bomb; the world could end any minute. Hedonism and the accelerated pace of pop culture came from this cosmic urgency. They might drop the bomb tomorrow, so let's party. By the 1970s, however, few knew just what the bomb *was*. Tippicano? The Battle of Culloden? It's history, fer chrissakes. The bomb *party*, however, goes on. The big bash that started in the fifties and really got going in the sixties—there was a war then, wasn't there?—was in and of itself way cool. Who needed a reason?

Punks added an ingenious twist to all of this impending annihilation. They behaved as if the nuclear holocaust had already taken place. The world was so badly fucked up, how much worse would it be if they *had* dropped the bomb? The bomb might actually serve a purpose. It might cleanse the world of the accumulated debris of the past, which was now clogging up everything, suffocating its children. Punks even *looked* like mutations. They were the radioactive rats who had survived the first strike.

Forget about politics or economics—they were of no concern to the lumpen hordes. And all this stuff about progress sounded suspiciously like Newspeak propaganda from *1984*. Progress was merely a slogan—"Progress is our most important product"—an absurd gimmick that only avaricious CEOs and public-relations hacks believed.

The Punk train had shunted off the main line of history anyway. They'd unplugged. They saw civilization as a twitching cadaver whose nervous system still functioned in a depressingly autonomic manner. But it was brain-dead, dead as a doornail, dead as a dodo.

5

The Zeitguy

NINETEEN SEVENTY-FIVE. FIVE YEARS HAD PASSED SINCE THE
Last New Thing. *Five years!* A lost generation wandering in
the wilderness, faceless hordes without a Moses to lead them
through Sinai to the Promised Land.

For Punks there was some urgency to this project. If they
did not come up with something soon, other commercially-
ground-out images would shape their generation. The music
industry wasn't exactly waiting around for the muse of fire to
strike. Actually, it wasn't all that unhappy with the way things
were. Business favors the steady state to the cyclical eruptions
of rock.

Teens in desperate need of a hit of the old sonic synthamesc may have been awaiting the descent from astral realms of the new god, but record-company executives weren't going to sit out the famine gnashing their teeth, wearing ruts in their Saxony plush carpets. No waiting around like gormless shepherds in their corporate pastures, anticipating the arrival of the new messiah, praying for the Next Big Thing. They wanted product. Now. Like any other business they wanted that product to come out in a steady and constant stream, but the music-biz need for controlled, orderly output is not conducive to the spasmodic, lurching nature of rock. So when the spirit wavered, the record company executives sold what was there.

> I HATE EVERYFING TO DO WIF TELEVISION; IT'S THE WORST, IT'S DEPRESSIN, TELEVISION. IT FRIGHTENS ME. THE WAY THEY FUCKIN KISS ARSE, YOU KNOW WHAT I MEAN? THE WAY THEY SAY: "AND NOW THE WONDERFUL THIS, AN THE WONDERFUL THE OTHER." THEY DON'T MEAN ONE FUCKIN WORD, YOU KNOW WHAT I MEAN? SO WHY DO IT?

What was there was terrifyingly bland and predictable. If something weren't done soon, the sound that would represent the era was ABBA. Allah preserve us in our wretchedness! Homogenized, extruded Europop. What a fucking nightmare.

Not to mention all those old records to repackage. K-tel's golden-oldie packages accounted for 30 percent of all records sold. The past was in danger of crushing the very life out of the present. Hits of the living dead! Vinyl zombies taking up all the oxygen! Jim Reeves, who'd died in the fifties, had a number-one album in 1975 with *40 Golden Hits*. We were meat for dead cowboys!

By mid-decade in England we had already gone through heavy metal, glam rock, two tone, disco, Northern soul, pub rock, skinhead ska, neo-mod, and thrash bands. Who would give this lost generation a face?

Perversely enough, a generation found its identity in someone who barely had one. He had been born John Simon Ritchie but often used his mother's maiden name, Beverley, as his surname, sometimes calling himself John, sometimes Simon. His *nom de Punk* was given to him by his friend John Lydon, and he lived his life according to a sex, drugs and rock 'n' roll movie scripted by Iggy Pop.

With his electroshock hair and Hammer horror-movie stare, Sid looked like the result of a ghastly experiment. And that's what he was—the mangled outcome of what had gone wrong with England. Everything about him said: "*You* did this to me!" He was the monster that was going to pull down the pillars. "*It made you a moron, a potential H-bomb. . . .*"

6
Early Sid

Punk's rewriting of history was to be Draconian. Whatever preceded them would be wiped off the face of the earth. *Après nous le déluge!* Like a selection committee at Noah's ark they'd embrace a few choice precursors and consign all others to oblivion. Punk public enemy number one was hippies. Whatever *they* did was to be avoided at all costs. Negative choice was the principle method of self-definition. No to astrology, tarot cards, patchouli, and brown rice.

Everything black or white. Very adolescent business this, but it came down to a matter of style. Scissors cut paper, rock crushes scissors, so it's axiomatic that style takes precedence over content. Style *is* content. What else *would* it be? For teenagers, posturing is of the essence.

British life swings between periods of hedonism and puritanism. Since the hippie ethic was one of willful pleasure-seeking, Punks would affect a perverse asceticism. But this presented them with a very thorny dilemma. To wit: What to do about the hippie catechism—sex, drugs, and rock 'n' roll (one of the most compelling catchphrases ever devised)? The three nested theses of rock. How was one to get around them?

The easiest of these to dispose of was sex. Big fucking deal! Punk high society dismissed the quasi-religious status of free love to "squelching sessions." Once you removed all the hippie greeting-card schmaltz and the Kama Sutra theology, what was it but a bit of the old in-out?

Drugs were, uh, just a wee bit harder to dispense with. Although the initial Punk pitch was "We don't take drugs," this Maginot Line fell almost instantly. Amphetamine sulfate was the drug of choice, as it had been for hippies and mods and beatniks and rockers and basically any other youth movement you could name. But acid was surprisingly common among Punks, too. Punks took acid probably more habitually than most hippies. For hippies LSD had been a sacrament; for Punks it was just another buzz.

The sacra-fuckin'-mental nature of LSD as proclaimed by such dodos as Timothy Leary and Richard Alpert (Baba Ram Dass, the old fart had taken to calling himself—can you credit it?) was fatuous, self-important bunk. *That* acid was something you took only in an appropriate setting—Mother Nature, tinkling bells, or the obligatory Grateful Dead concert. What spineless cretins! All this transcendental business was just bollocks. Didn't they realize LSD was just another teenage thrill?

The idea that some pharmaceutical company in Switzerland was going to come up with a drug that would reveal the mysteries of the cosmos, what a joke! Take a drug and see God! How fucking credulous could you get? Go ask Alice, shithead.

Punks condemned the mindless pleasure-seeking hippies with the moral indignation of a Savonarola while proceeding to indulge in those very excesses themselves. The Punk front was abstemious, but Punk practice was business as usual with a slight change in the emphasis: drugs (lots), rock 'n' roll (if possible), and sex (so long as you don't mind if I sleep through it).

7

An Experiment in Social Engineering

Wif me, above all else, looks is wot matters. I was always vainglorious in that respect. I willingly make confession of it. Even durin me most fucked-up periods I was ever ponderin me image, thumbin through all the flash an glossy mags for the latest à la mode. It is holy scriptures wif me. 'Ow the world perceives you, that's vital, y'know. Takes a load of fuckin work to look like me! There's many don't understand this.

THE QUEST FOR STYLE WENT ON. THE SEARCH FOR A UNIFIED theory took on an urgent and frantic aspect; for the most part nothing more than an ongoing costume party. Pirates, old proletariat, granddad shirts, loon pants, glitter. Well, it just wouldn't do. It was scrappy and cheesy, and what did all this dressing-up *mean*, anyway? It only underlined the fact that the blank generation was feckless and derivative, their age void and without form.

The Sex Pistols' story proper begins as a gothic fairy tale involving two manifesto-mongering fashion sorcerers with odd ideas such as "the moral purpose of clothes" and an alarming line of goods. With their mildly radical ideas about social engineering and their kinky streetwear, Malcolm McLaren and Vivienne Westwood opened Sex at number 430 on the King's Road in 1974.

> **I 'ATE FILMS BECAUSE PEOPLE 'AVE TO ACT PARTS IN 'EM. IMAGINE THAT, PLAYIN PEOPLE WHO THEY IS NOT. DO YOU KNOW WHAT I MEAN? AN IT'S PRETENSE, IT'S LIES, IT'S JUST SHIT. IT BUILDS FINGS UP TO BE WOT THEY CLEARLY IS NOT.**

McLaren had found his road to Damascus on the corner of Edith Grove when he was accosted by a man who was struck by his Lurex trousers. This was the kind of epiphany you had in England in the seventies. In a hidebound and constricted society such as the U.K., fashion is one of the few areas where you can reinvent yourself.

McLaren had gone through various style-obsessed cults and been disappointed in them all. The most disheartening of his ventures being the teds, English rockers who dressed in Edwardian suits, listened to fifties rock, and adhered to a strict moral code. Unfortunately for McLaren they turned out to be even more reactionary and close-minded than repressed British society in general.

But McLaren's intuition was dead on the mark. The fifties held the key. What was it about the fifties? They were repressed and conformist, therefore hot and rebellious. It was the friction in the fifties thing that attracted him. As a charter member of the Order of Manic Hegelians, McLaren saw tension as the engine, if not of history, of its bastard child, pop culture.

Pop subcultures all had one thing in common—they

were cults devoted to a frantic, committed lifestyle. Three decades of comic strips, louche Hollywood glamour, rock 'n' roll glitter, street flash, and pop *kitsch und quatsch* grinding away at prevailing taste had inverted what was left of high style. The hipoisie now dabbled in garish and fantastic camp.

If McLaren and Westwood were archaeologists of pop culture excavating an industrial Ur of the Chaldees, their area of study required no specialized knowledge. It was all right there. Pop culture was bomb culture; its history was in the air.

To draw a bead on guerrilla style, clothes would need sting. Like dentists searching for a nerve, McLaren and Westwood probed the national tooth. What were the touchiest spots? They identified two: fetishwear and Nazi regalia. Here was maximum menace, putting into relief sexual hypocrisy, class prejudices, and British delusions of grandeur.

> **Malcolm, bless his black heart, knows 'ow to milk the media for all it's worth. In the office I hear 'im spoutin 'is mouf off abawt 'ow we is a conceptual band, wif which I heartily concur because wot else would we be? We can't play, we don't 'afta make records, we don't even 'afta appear anywhere. All we 'ave to do is create outrage, which we is well equipped to do. Still, wot a wanker. 'Ee's a megalomaniac in the purest sense, 'is most endearin quality being 'is capacity of turning disasters to good use—an then turnin 'em back into disasters again!**

McLaren's guru was clearly Andrew Loog Oldham, the razor-sharp malchick mod manager of the Rolling Stones.

Both were thoroughly mediated personalities with a mania for mythologizing and low-culture posturing. Like Oldham, McLaren was obsessed with fashion as a sort of gnostic key to the mechanics of culture. Whether the collar should be round or pointed or a cuff have a half- or quarter-inch showing, these were matters of almost theological importance to Sir Andrew.

McLaren and Westwood went one step further, confounding style and morality and turning Lenin's axiom "Ethics will be the aesthetics of the future" inside out. Style, when scrupulously applied, *was* morality. This was straight out of the bible of modernist aesthetics. McLaren and Westwood were true believers in the Bauhaus credo that design itself could reform society. At its core, Punk style is the result of modernist art-school design hysteria interacting with working-class street armor. An elitist enterprise from the get-go.

Your average Brit is clueless in matters of style. As a type, the frumpy Englishman holidaying on the Continent is a source of endless amusement to the savvy Eurosuaves. While this is true of the general population, there are two segments of Brit society that have a very keen fashion sense. There's the upper crust with their Savile Row bespoke tailors. You know, cavalry tweed twill trousers, demob pinstripes, Aquascutum macs. Not to your average hipster's taste, perhaps, but it's nothing if not *thought out*. Then, at the other end of the spectrum, you've got your underclass fashion plates, the barrow boys and all-night ravers, who are equally style wise. They think nothing of dropping their entire salary on one flash outfit and throwing it in the dustbin the next day.

This spiffy crowd gave birth to teds, mods, skinheads, etcetera.

Both are essentially class uniforms; clothes for these two groups function as a sort of carapace, but whereas the Savile Row crowd are fustian reactionaries in matters of style—the costume hadn't changed significantly in a hundred years—the Cockney contingent were ferociously contemporary, hence the mods in the sixties, short for modernists. Mod, like all rock movements, had a stylistic worldview. Clothes, music, style were all of a piece, and it was this cohesiveness that McLaren and Westwood wanted to re-create and somehow fuse onto the existential ferocity of fifties rock.

Stylistically, the pop machine had stalled after mod. Mod was immediately cannibalized and debased by Carnaby Street (viz such travesties as *The Mod Squad*). And with the mass bohemia of the sixties came another set of trendies: the Antique Market gypsy tatterdemalion of the King's Road loons. This pre-Raphaelite flummery, which came straight from the ye olde William Morris tradition of florid neo-medievalism, was started by art-school students.

Well, McLaren had been to art school, too, and had a keen sense of style. But he wasn't interested in fancy dress costumes. No, that sort of froufrou was anathema to McLaren and Westwood. They were moralists. They would have none of this dressing-up business! They wanted fashion to operate like a loaded gun. Into *the look* they injected the rhetoric of late sixties radical politics, sexual fetishism, pop history.

Westwood and McLaren's pursuit of an obnoxious chic meshed effortlessly with the needs of the kids who hung out at Sex. Locating areas of maximum aggravation to adults was their principle activity. Around them and their shop, Sex, formed a cluster of youthful malcontents. Sex was a nursery where children could indulge in pop acts of transformation. New monsters safely hatched here. Misfits who wanted to change the world or just to belong to a club of rejects (in the marginal industry of pop this was possible). A motley collection of perverts and primadonnas straight out of Warhol. Gays, drug addicts, sexual delinquents, neo-mods, and curious lads and lasses who were simply attracted to the bizarre and tantalizing merchandise.

At Sex only clothing that bristled with provocative meanings was considered. Clothes didn't have to have specific meanings. Ambivalence was just as good. BE REASONABLE, DEMAND THE IMPOSSIBLE mixed with Frog agitprop slogans. *Prênez vos désires, pour la realité, À bas le Coca-Cola!*

Symbols, insignia. Signs without meaning—hollow signifiers—were also perfectly acceptable. All part of a bricolage mentality, the piecing together of fragments.

T-shirts speaking in tongues, patches canceling each other out, clothing muttering unspeakable things. The density of reference was boggling. *Years* it would take to unravel! To your average passerby on his way to work it was a blitz of messages—all hostile.

In the beginning, Punks would define themselves by what they hated, and what they hated constituted a considerable list. The names of the despised were published not in a magazine but on a T-shirt designed by McLaren and Jamie Reid. The "Hates" (a selected list):

(HATES:) Television (not the group)/Mick
Jagger/The Liberal Party / John Betjeman/
Parking tickets/*19, Honey, Harpers, Vogue*, in fact
all magazines that treat their readers as
idiots/Bryan Ferry/Salvador Dali/Anthony
Haden-Guest/Grey skies/Dirty books that aren't
all that dirty/*Top of the Pops*/John Dunbar/Take
Six/Good Fun Entertainment when it's not all
that good or fun/All those fucking saints. . . .

And on and on—some fifty odd names.

Plus another fifty or so "Loves". But even their heroes
were elected principally for perverse reasons. Sex profes-
sionals, hard rockers, terrorists.

This wasn't a T-shirt as is generally understood by the
word—a white cotton shirt bearing some fatuous sentiment
or commercial logo—this was a manifesto, the sort of thing
that used to get tacked to the doors of cathedrals. Not one of
those dopey trend-tracking year-end lists of who's in and
who's out compiled by glossy magazines, but a thesis with a
specific target in mind.

Hates on the left and Loves on the right. This would
be the blueprint for the Punk *reich*. Polarization was the
essence of the manifesto t-shirt: "You're gonna wake up one
morning and *know* what side of the bed you've been lying
on." It was in your face—like some rabid Electrical Workers
Union foreman.

Malcolm was in awe of symbolism. Symbolism was sexy.
Polyphrenic T-shirts! Talking, *shrieking* outfits. All at once

you'd have: anarchist ideology + situationist sloganeering + sexual fetishism + Nazi insignia. Loaded, antisocial messages flashing like a strobe . . . cult . . . taboo . . . violence . . . disturbance . . . threat . . . perversion. And all saying: We hate you and everything you stand for.

What if history were not about battles and senators and Great Ideas but . . . fashion? And why not? Every other coterie has its claim to be the *real* history, the secret history of the world. Art! Music! Metaphysics! They all had their esoteric claims to be the true subterranean stream that nourished civilization. Each thought *they* were the thread on which those treaties and riots were strung like so many beads. And drugs! Of course! All those underground papers claiming hallucinogens as the true shifters of the paradigm. Christ was really into magic mushrooms. But you knew that.

After all, isn't fashion the ancient secret language of the street? Walkabout hieroglyphics telegraphing ominous signals to the cognoscenti: short hemlines—war's about to be declared; granny dresses—get ready for the next depression. Women have understood this since the beginning of time. Fashion being all the more effective a discipline for being despised. Lower than, say, furniture design, in the hierarchy of creative genius. Subversive because dismissed as trivial. Subliminal.

All right, it's preposterous, like a button maker saying all history can be reduced to buttons. "Did you know that in the sixteenth century the first four-holed button led to the Hundred Years War?" But who said any of this was reasonable?

It was a question Malcolm and Vivienne had to ask themselves daily: "Are we being unreasonable *enough?*" So their idea—to start a revolution based on clothes. What jokers! Son of Andy Warhol, indeed. McLaren was Warhol Lite. The quest for unreason, the long and winding road ending, yes, right there on the King's Road. This is where rampant modernism, abnormal psychology, the unrestrained teen libido, and rock 'n' roll found themselves in sync.

The clothes sold at Sex were spectacularly outré. Get yer rubber T-shirts! Try our fifties trousers getup! Vinyl halter tops, this week's special! Swastika armbands, SS hankies, gestapo buddy rings. Dog collars as common and chic as a string of pearls.

Some of the clientele—balding gents in pinstriped suits and bowler hats popping in on their lunch hour to slip into a pair of rubber underpants—clearly weren't buying this stuff to aggravate their parents. Heads of multinational cartels who like to lick toilet bowls, crawl along on all fours while Mistress Grimm flicks their bare bottom with a cat-o-nine-tails. One can *explain* this—a lengthy psychological study using many unpronounceable German words would do the trick. But let's face it, it's still unreasonable as hell.

Put this together with that other pit of unreason, the Nazis, and you're safely beyond the pale. This is the deep end of irrationality. Swastika armbands and S&M gear at seven o'clock in the morning at the Holburn tube station will wake people up like nobody's business.

Although McLaren/Westwood usually eschewed clothing that was camp for its own sake, many of the kids attracted to Sex were well up camp tree. There were Liza Minnelli, Joel Grey, and David Bowie clones; all stars with personas in quotation marks. Transvestites, girls on the game. Androgynous changelings, blank slates. Dad's a chartered accountant, but the child is wild.

And the Bromley contingent—misfits, bisexuals, nonsexuals. Pubescent freaks for whom the only besetting sin was normalcy. It's like the Firesign Theater routine where hipster commissars drop copies of *Naked Lunch* on the last pockets of straight resistance.

For a revolution—even a tempest in a teapot like Punk—you need uniforms, badges, and a nasty little cult to go with it. Yes, the very thing. Some little sociosexual pseudo–death squad sect bristling with so many signs that you can't really tell what's going on. All you know is that the whole of the twentieth century is blowing up in your face. Some yob, fulminating with hostility and all those poisonous, omnidirectional signifiers like so many bristles on a porcupine and all saying: "I'm a fucking bloody mess and *you're* responsible. I'm a victim, victim, victim, and because of what *you've* done, what society's done, what the whole bleedin' twentieth century's done to me. . . ."

I FINK I'M GONNA SMASH YOUR FACE IN WIF ME BICYCLE CHAIN!

And thinking about it, all what history's done to this poor lad, what a bleedin' insult it is and all, you end up feeling sorry for the twitchy, green-haired little troll. Nietzsche killed off God, Van

Gogh replaced God with nature, Jackson Pollock replaced nature with art (and himself). God, if you listened to the twaddle going around, was Eric Clapton. What else did you expect but insults from these kids? What had we done to them, the poor sods?

Volatile teens were drawn irresistibly to the numbingly splenetic re-

DOWN HAVIN A DRINK (OR SEVEN) AT CLUB LOUISE, CHRISSIE SCRIBBLIN AWAY OVER IN THE CORNER 'ER NAUGHTY NEIGHBOR QUOTES FOR PENTHOUSE FORUM. 'ELLO BILLY, YOU KNOW BILLY IDOL, DON'TCHA? THE PROLEPTIC ADAM ANT POSTURIN AS USUAL, GHOST DRUMMER MICK JONES AN SIOUXSIE A'COURSE. 'OO ELSE'S HERE TONIGHT?

galia of delinquency. It was all in the mix. Polymorphous sexuality and random hostility. The idea was to look like a cartoon. Broad outlines, jagged eye makeup, *Clockwork Orange* boiler suits.

Rock 'n' roll is an accommodating medium. Any number of styles or attitudes can be grafted on to it and (for the most part) adhere and become part of it. What doesn't stick—raga-rock, *musique concrète*, etcetera—clearly didn't belong there in the first place.

Nihilism and aberrant sex were irresistible to the dispossessed yobs from the council houses. Almost immediately, Sex attracted a pack of disturbed and disruptive youth. Among them the future Johnny Rotten and Sid Vicious.

When McLaren saw the foppishly transvestite and musically inept New York Dolls, his eyes lit up. A group whose cardinal quality was style, the Dolls almost had it made but they committed the unforgivable faux pas of having long hair and wearing platform shoes.

Hadn't rock 'n' roll begun with posing in the mirror? Rock style seemed to be a corollary to the music. Or, thought McLaren, maybe it was the other way around. But first there was all that muso mystification to contend with. All those snotty brats who talked barre chords and diminished sevenths. Clearly loathsome little megalomaniacs who wouldn't take all that kindly to being clotheshorses for a kinky boutique on the King's Road.

After trying unsuccessfully to promote the Dolls, McLaren returns to England with the idea of forming a similar group who'll wear his clothes and advertise the shop. Enter the Sex Pistols. In one of the most bizarre twists in the history of rock, *the* archetypal rock group begins as a promotional gimmick to bring people into a boutique to buy torn T-shirts.

McLaren had envisioned his hypothetical group as a camp version of the Bay City Rollers. Your basic bubblegum rock group, in other words. The genius was in the name: the Sex Pistols. It was surreal in a deadpan way, something radically different in the endless rock-group name game. Nothing like those tired old dangling modifiers thought up by psychedelic bands. It might almost be said that the name, like the opening words of the Gospel According to John, brought everything else into existence. Kids hearing it for the first time were mesmerized. Writers at the English music weeklies were struck dumb at the sound.

McLaren was a trend spotter, a stirrer-up of things, but by his very nature uncommitted. His was a windsock philosophy. You used everything that came to hand and then discarded it, claiming, preferably, that your previous stance had been a scam. As soon as something succeeded, he tired of it. He'd proved his point. On to the next hustle!

As the impresario of Punk, McLaren presented himself as a conjurer pulling breathtaking sleights of hand out of a cocked hat. The Great Oz, the confidence man, the capitalist incarnation of the Trickster of folklore (Anansi, Coyote, Monkey) the latest in a long line of illusionists and snake-oil salesmen of rock. It began with Colonel Tom Parker, a salesman for a patent medicine called Hatacol before he discovered Elvis.

McLaren began providing rehearsal space for a group of kids calling themselves the Swankers who hung around the store. They formed the core of the Sex Pistols: Paul Cook (drums), Steve Jones (guitar), and eventually Glen Matlock (bass). They were dedicated musos who took the gig seriously and eventually learned to play their instruments. For these three there was never any of the aggressive amateurism that later became a badge of honor for Johnny Rotten and Sid Vicious.

The McLaren doctrine said that he could have turned any bunch of yobs, given a certain innate aggro and flash, into the Sex Pistols. That was the *point* of the Sex Pistols. They were ciphers you could dress up and point in the right direction.

If the Sex Pistols had consisted only of the original core

members—Cook, Jones, Matlock—McLaren's claims to have been the manipulator of the band, the Great Svengali, might be more plausible. This group was easily handled. They were musicians pure and simple. The usual crew—musos looking for gigs, a record contract, in it for the "piss-up and the birds after the show." These guys were just glad not to be apprentice bricklayers and electricians' mates. But once John Lydon entered the picture everything changed. With Sid the frame shattered.

> **Malcolm, the fifth member of the band? Err. How vile. 'Ee never even turns up to the gigs. Oi, the band has never been dependent on Malcolm, that ol toss-bag. I 'ate the geezer. I'd smash 'is face in quite 'appily. I depend on 'im for exactly nuffin. 'Ee gave me a free T-shirt once years ago an 'ee once gave me a fiver. Also I stole a tenner off 'im a little while ago. An that's all, loathsome creature.**

'Ave you ever been subjected to a interview by the musical press? It is a experience I can assure you you would gladly forgo, bein somewot akin to a copper arskin you where you has been at 9:30 of a Thursday evenin.

Viz: What do you consider your musical priorities?
Wot a load of bollocks! An wif a straight face, mind. They don't 'alf arsk some stoopid rubbish. But Vivienne an Malcolm 'ave taught us well in the Academy of Naughty Outfits. Intonin the Malcolmspeak wif which I 'ave bin embued, I goes on to further obfuscate: "The Pistols, like deviant sex, is a symbolic fing." In uvver words the Pistols is symbols, mate, an symbols is inviolate from criticism, ain't they? Or bloody well should be. Next question.

I see you're wearing both a swastika an a dog collar. Aren't these somewht contradictory?
All a question of sartorial dialectics, innit, mate? Usin the iconology of fascism an fetishism is by the way of implyin distance from the normal, right? Normal behavior, normal politics, normal bollocks. Which is why we is saints of the anti-cult, old darlin, an while we is on the subject, would you care, perhaps, for a jack of pharmeceutical heroin an a little toilet discipline?

8

The Blank Generation

GROUND ZERO FOR PUNK WAS THAT NIGHT THE SEX PISTOLS PERformed at the 100 Club. Tuesday the eleventh of May, 1976. Remember that date, children. Where it all began.

Momentary freeze-frame as the lead singer makes his entrance. Lydon's penny-dreadful poltergeist. Menacing meningitis eyes looming out. Almost brush up against the surface of the screen. Twitching alien antennae. Pull back reflexively. The clip runs. Lydon in motion. Little bits of London fright legend stitched together and given breathless life. A full-blown Dickensian demon of the slums. But it's becoming a species of diorama. The Rotten character can only devolve from here into self-parody. It is immaculate but resistant to amplification or modulation, like a grand Old Vic actor playing a villain in a Jacobean tragedy. The same award-winning performance every night for those expensive seats in the stalls. So predictable and *baw-ring!*

The seminal emblems of Punk are here—safety pins, spiked hair, gobbing, the pogo. Telepathy and tension. Note: First recorded incident of pogoing in the U.K. Sid starts jumping up and down on the spot with excitement, bashing into people. Ther ya go, a new fuckin dance craze. Sid started it off and John started the safety pins off and between them they were responsible for jump-starting the revolution.

Under the Punk regime, all tourism would stop. Visits to the Tower of London, bobbies, Buckingham Palace, the drippy Royals. Exterminate the fuckin' wallies! All those kitsch coronation plates, hideous Prince Charles mugs with his ears as handles! "Barbie Swan Coach coming in May"—*raus!* Fergie and Andrew, a tawdry, tarty soap opera. The Prince of Wales, a human tampon. Off with their heads!

The end of England. Decline and fall of. End of history, why not? *Novus ordo seclorum.* All the new creatures take on *noms de Punk*, names that boast they've been remade in the image of the new age. Lydon is given the name Rotten by Paul Cook on account of his green, suppurating teeth. Sid gets his name from Rotten. "I called him Sid after my pet hamster. Vicious came later, after the Lou Reed song."

Like many other subcultures—fauves, beatniks—slurs and insults are taken as pet names, pseudonyms flaunted as a badge of pride. Rotten and Sid are shining examples of the insult turned on its head.

The "Rotten" taunt seems never to have bothered

Lydon although he hated being addressed by his "stage name." He used the gap between himself and his character to his own advantage. He could unzip Rotten and return to his old self when it suited him.

But where Lydon acted Johnny Rotten, Beverley *became* Sid Vicious. Vicious took over John Beverley body and soul, and the Vicious incubus was all the more insidious for seeming to be his real self. At first in the eyes of outsiders, and eventually to himself.

Johnny Rotten was suitably outrageous, a breath of fresh air. His bracing opinions were of a piece with the Sex Pistols' imagery. This was exactly what you'd expect a group who looked like the Sex Pistols to say: "Culture is a hokey fraud. We're near the end of the twentieth century—who needs it anymore?" *Awright!*

Rotten's act consisted of parodic disdain for the audience. A wickedly effective posture because it monopolizes all the available roles and forces his critics into the role of gratuitous, envious outsiders. A right mimic that Johnny Lydon, with his American accent, schoolboy snarl, Irish brogue, and Somerset rural. A host of speakers jostling inside him, a bolshy, turbulent crowd of Rottens. His name was legion.

I dropped outta school shortly afta finaglin a scholarship (didn't know abawt the dole yet) an used the money to start up me own illicit business the nature of which I must wifhold in order to protect the guilty sods as was involved wif me. It was at 'Ackney Technical College that I met Lydon. We were right thick cunts we were, 'im an me. 'Ee was the vilest geezer I evah met—all misshapen, no air, 'unchback, flat feet. Everybody 'ated 'im. Everybody 'ated me. We 'ated each uvver, too, but nobody else would talk to us, so we'd just get drunk an criticize each uvver. 'Ee used to tell people 'ee 'ad to cut 'is piles awf wif a razor blade because they were hangin out 'is pants an they'd believe 'im. 'Ee used to tell 'em niggers ad 'air on the roofs of their mouths an they believed that, too.

9

How the Hippie Reich
Was Undone

THERE IS ONLY ONE GROUP OF PEOPLE WHOM ADOLESCENTS DIS-
dain more than their parents and that is the previous generation. The selfish giants who would not make way. It didn't
matter how hip or cool the preceding teen *reich* had been—
or thought it was—it had to be overthrown by the next generation.

Hippies! On the one hand, proto-Punks were furious
that hippies had said they'd change the world and hadn't. On
the other hand, Punks had come to the equally appalling
conclusion that hippies *had* taken over the world. At least
those parts of the world any teenager would care about:
music and fashion. What a horror! And now the old farts

wanted to stop *time*. The Old Year, the ancien régime of sixties rock, was The Thing That Would Not Die. The land withered, the crops failed and all because the lardy old Lear in a sheepskin coat would not give up his throne. Where was the Fisher King who would revive the desolate landscape? The Seven Lean Years were upon us. Joni Mitchell and James Taylor like some wet and weedy minstrelsy sang the songs, but the seasons refused to change.

> **TOSSED OUTTA LINDA ASHBY'S AND WAS OBLIGED TO RESIDE TEMPORARILY WIF ME MUM. NANCE AN MA VICIOUS GET ON FAMOUSLY, A'COURSE. AN IF YOU BELIEVES THAT I WILL TELL YOU ANUVVER ONE. BUT NOW ME MUM 'AS A NEW BOYFRIEND SO WE 'AVE TO HIGHTAIL IT OUTTA 'ERE.**

The sense of being born too late is an endemic condition among teenagers. That all coolness has gone before them is axiomatic, but hippies had the supreme gall to rub it in. Not only had they, the coming-of-age-in-the-seventies, missed out on what was clearly the hippest, most exciting time for any teenager to have been alive, they were constantly *reminded* of it. Sid Vicious—especially vexed by this as the child of a hippie-era mother—turned it into a Punk taunt: "Remember the summer of love?" After you'd heard it a few times the whole idea of a summer of love took on an oleaginous quality.

When you tried to envision this legendary era populated by tahini-encrusted, overweight nudists in ponytails and paisley—your parents!—it conjured up a truly revolting scene.

Something like a drugged-out game show, a sort of psychedelic *Dating Game*.

Hippies (especially their politico brethren, Yippies) went on and on about the social change that must be wrought. Civil rights, end the war! But to Punks such political trumpeting was absurd—more aberrant rhetoric. Further proof, if any were needed, of hippie gullibility. Hippies had actually believed they could change the world! Get *out*! Teenagers changing the world was a James Dean movie gone megalomaniacal. Like *Wild in the Streets*, where anyone over thirty is consigned to a concentration camp, and the voting age is lowered to fourteen.

By far the dopiest notion of all—and a dearly cherished hippie belief—was that rock 'n' roll would be the means for this universal transformation. Pop songs? Really? What dimwits! What Pecksniffian cant! This was entertainment, fer chrissakes.

Lydon: " 'Anarchy in the U.K.' was about musical anarchy. I don't think you can be a political rock 'n' roll band. It's a loser stance."

Punk would mimic revolutionary rhetoric but only in its inverse form. It wouldn't look good for the nihilist image of the Blank Generation to imply that it really wanted to *change* anything. Do we look to you like people who care?

Hippie/Punk feuds took on many of the characteristics of conflicting religious sects within the same rock 'n' roll sacrament. The theological point at issue was the just use of the true faith of the youth culture and its syncretic religion: rock 'n' roll.

Idolators! Rock wasn't just some tool to be used for social change, rock was the Ark of the Covenant. It was the sacred trust of all the rebels without a cause—the only possible rebellion. Any revolution *with* a cause was doomed, contaminated from the word go by engaging with a corrupt adult world.

> '00 SEZ YA CAN'T FIGHT WIF WOMEN? WHERE'S THE EQUALITY IN IT IF YOU GONNA START MAKIN ALL THEM TWADDLIN DISTINCTIONS? THEY CAN FIGHT FUCKIN BETTER THAN MOST GUYS, I CAN TELL YOU.

Half-baked hippie transcendentalism had for Punks a buffoonish quality about it. Sanctimonious hippies chanting mantras and intoning outlandish spells was a grotesque image. Weren't these the same idiots who'd tried to levitate the Pentagon?

Sure, noble life-enhancing things had come out of the hippie experience—ecology for instance—but the very worthiness of this sort of thing made it suspect.

And hippie taste! Paisley and lace, pre-Raphaelite gloom, lava lamps, black light, Peter Max posters, balloon lettering. All that psychedelic kitsch and quatsch. It was all so twee and weedy compared to the stripped-down, machine-tooled esthetics of Punk with its ransom-note lettering and black leather. Not that Punk eschewed kitsch; Punks enthusiastically embraced anything that tasteful people considered in bad taste. Kitsch was absorbed by Punk in quotation marks, as irony, as camp, *knowingly* incorporated as artifacts of a kitsch culture. But hippie kitsch was beyond the pale. As dowdy and frumpy as your auntie's antimacassar. "These people were caricatures," says Rotten. "With their silly scarves thrown over milk crates to make things look ever so nice. The smell of joss sticks. They all sat on cushions on the floor."

Hippies had become chronically Pollyannaish. Bourgeois goody-goodies. No self-respecting rocker would ever stoop to such maudlin depths.

Look what happened to them, fer chrissakes. Time caught up with them. Too successful for their own good—all those hippie entrepreneurs loping into record companies with their tie-dyed dreams. The more successful your revolution, the sooner you turn into what you set out to destroy.

The Great Beast that had once pulsed with a million neon suns was now exhausted, a slobbering hulk, its bloated carcass deposited outside the city of Babylon, rotting in the sun. Some saw apocalyptic signs in rock's imminent demise.

The dirge started with the QWERTies—rock critics, music journalists, whatever you want to call them—wailing in a low strangled moan: "It's over! All is lost!" like a bloody Greek chorus. Rock writers, Rotten's "typewriter gods," had begun saying it, the forbidden thing, with masochistic relish. The terrible words *IS ROCK DEAD?* began showing up in cover lines. Had it come to this?

10

Sermon to a
Wayward Flock

BUT NO AMOUNT OF WHIMSY CAN CONCEAL THE HORROR OF ALL that energy and ecstasy transmuted into real estate. Heresies of the true faith! Everything about it—long-term investment, annual yields—a travesty. An obscenity, O my brothers! The corpse that gets up and does a jig.

Prince Rupert Lowenstein, money manager to the Stones, juggling vaporous paper entities, holding companies, phantom corporations, frozen assets. This is what became of "Satisfaction," children. Keith's Bar Keys horn-riff guitar turned into a mini-mall in Omaha. "Stairway to Heaven" a B.J.'s megastore.

All those slick blues runs, the million-dollar riffs. That

flaky virtuosity, the fastest-guitar-alive shit. Didn't they know rock wasn't about becoming a fretboard Paganini, about how many notes you could cram in? Lissen, you sods in your tapestry jerkins and crushed velvet pants, don't you know this is the twentieth fuckin' century? Modernism had been all about *un*learning. Forget the jiggery-pokery, the bag of tricks, the clever-lad devices. How could you ever think the sacred cow of rock could be cornswaddled with *arpeggios*? The whole point—fools!—was to regain the purity of the original vision: a flaming black pig screaming down the streets of the mind.

How could you stray so far from the true path as to think that tumescent zoom could be caught in overdub upon overdub? Hadn't Little Richard, Howlin' Wolf, Otis Redding, James Brown, Jerry Lee Lewis, Eddie Cochran—the real guys, the Progenitors—recorded *whole albums*, mixed and everything and outta there, in three hours?

Now groups were taking a year and a half to make an album! There were 32-track studios. Dear bleeding Jesus, how could they ever expect to harness the mad bull of teen paroxysm in those airless labyrinths? Hundreds of thousands of dollars mixing, sweetening, *perfecting*. . . . Perfecting that which should not *be* perfect. Madness! Delusion! Tricked by the smoothing, sweetening devils.

If Punks glommed on to one person as the target of their scorn it was Sir Mick. He was symbolic of all that had turned sour in Denmark. The love-hate thing with Jagger took on mythic dimensions—the *Epic of Gilgamesh* reenacted on the King's Road. Gilgamesh versus the Bull of Heaven! Jagger's standing in rock had somehow achieved canonical status like

48

Greenwich mean time or the missionary position. The established norm from which they would deviate.

JUNE 11, 1977. Have a little visit wif the Daily Wanker today. "I'll probably die by the time I reach twenty-five, but I'll have lived the way I wanted to." I expostulate to Jack Spratt. Wot a prat! Trying to draw me out, all sly-like. Was I violent an fings like that, an if I did this an that. All very subtle, designed to a person of low intelligence, obviously such as myself. So I tells 'im the exact opposite of what 'ee wants to 'ear. I tells 'im wot a nice intellectual boy I was an I wouldn't dream of doing anyfing like that an I 'ad pet 'ampsters an fings like that, you know what I mean? Made myself seem like butter wouldn't melt in me mouth an he fuckin' fell for it as well. They're just so thick they wouldn't know a string quartet from a string vest. Make me physically ill. Grown-ups ave just got no intelligence at all. As soon as you grow up you might as well kill yourself, which I strongly advocate. I intend to live up to me philosophy as well, which is why I say in all earnestness I will not live past twenty-five. You won't catch me doin 'Amlet Prince of Denmark on ice at the Crystal Palace. I 'ave me pride.

Why Sir Mick? Surely Paul McCartney would have been a more appropriate culprit for the pillory. But McCartney wasn't a useful mark—he was beneath contempt. Too wet and schmaltzy to be a worthy target for Punk wrath. The real bogeyman was Mick Jagger.

Why this unhealthy obsession with the transgressions of

Sir Mick? Because he could have done it right and hadn't. He'd sloped off instead with a bunch of wallies and poncey aristos.

Bowie, for serpentine reasons, was immune to criticism. For one thing most of them had *been* Bowie fans. The Thin White Duke, when deconstructed, was actually a syncretic neo-Jagger. But whereas Sir Mick now stood for everything rank and decadent, you would be hard pressed to say exactly *what* Bowie stood for.

Bowie was the master illusionist, the chameleon king. He was inscrutable. Like the Doppler effect, you didn't know where the source was. He was a little like the alien he played in *The Man Who Fell to Earth*. Every six months or so he morphed. Transvestite, extraterrestrial, dandy, glam—you could never get a fix on him. Bowie was the perfect idol for an amorphous era, and the perfect star for the interregnum. After all the bombastic *gesamtkunstwerks* of late-sixties rock, it was a relief to have an *entertainer*, a rock Noel Coward.

In the end Bowieism, if permitted to prevaricate indefinitely, would be held against them. In the Punk version of *It's a Wonderful Life*, the avenging angel might say: "You, Johnny Rotten, and you, Sid Vicious, saw this happening and you stood by and did nothing—as this plague of blandness swept the world, blighting the harvest, killing off the firstborn with its supermarket click-track drone. You have betrayed future ages of rockers and your names shall live in infamy!"

Scaly aliens with skin problems and bad teeth scan the planet. Their hipnosity Geiger counters, pointed at the mid-1970s, crackle with static. *Hah! Foolish earthlings stunned into immobility by Europap have become slaves of the palindromic ABBA. Swedoid replicants have hypnotized Earth cretins. Prepare to invade.*

In truth, of course, Sid *loved* ABBA. He would, if he'd thought of it himself, kept one of

WOT MALCOLM MISJUDGES 'ERE IS THAT THE FAR-RIGHT FUCKIN CHRISTIAN WANKERS WOULD EVEN KNOW OF US. DO YOU FINK PAT BUCHANAN LISSENS TO PUNK RECORDS? GET AWAY! WE IS TOO FAR OUT OF THEIR FIELD OF VISION TO NOTICE.

their turds in a bottle around his neck like the drag queen in *Priscilla, Queen of the Desert*. When he ran into them at the airport in Stockholm, he tried to kiss one of the girls' hands. They recoiled in horror. Thought *he* was the alien.

Meanwhile . . . in garages and basements across the land, kids were tinkering with that hypothetical hot rod of sound—yearning transmitted through the brutal thrust of a machine.

11

What Sid Understood

THE *UMMAH*, THE TRIBAL HIVE, WAS FORMING AROUND—WHAT else?—bands. The enigmatic Viv Albertine said she had one. Well, *could* have one. We'll just nip home and knock one to- gether. The Flowers of Romance they called it. In Punk, anyone could form a band. No experience necessary. In the December 1976 issue of the "Strangler-zine," *Sideburns*, there was a do-it-yourself kit for Punk rockers. A chart showing three chords—A, E, and G—and adding "NOW FORM A BAND." It was *that* easy.

With Punk, rock 'n' roll had been reduced to its most basic pulse. It was again easy to play—like skiffle, the jug- band music with which the Beatles began. Rock needs these periodic returns to *reductio ad crudum*. What rock doesn't want is more Paganinis. Just plug directly into the main-line teen valve and let whatever's bottled up blast through.

Beyond the three-chord initiation was the rock barre chord which involves barre-ing the top fret and often eliminating the middle note as well (ask a guitar player). If the archetypal rock barre chord reduced playing rock 'n' roll to its crudest form, rock bass-playing was even more rudimentary. You're playing single notes, and on the fast numbers thrumming percussively—like playing a drum. A drum and a drone.

Sid's bass-playing in the Flowers of Romance (and six months later in the Sex Pistols) was the lowest common denominator—pure rhythm pulse, getting the note and *drumming* on it. Pedaling straight 8s. If there are four beats to a bar, then "pedaling" adds in the "and," as in "one *and* two *and* three *and* four and." Total, pure drive, like the Ramones. Dee Dee Ramone, for instance, played the chords on the root note of the chord and just pumped away. This is your basic Punk bass.

Before I started playin I never really noticed the bass—couldn't tell the bloody fing from a piano, mate. I 'ear records as just a wall of sound. I'd 'ave to fink carefully before pickin anyfing out. It's like reggae, which I do fancy quite a lot as it 'appens, although I have never been able to suss exackly wot it is.

I never quite find out wot fings are, y'know wot I mean?

Sid's all-purpose riff was a bump-and-grind bass line, a rhythmic pattern worn into his synapses like a wheel rut. Essentially a cartoony garage-band riff from the Ramones' "I Don't Wanna Go Down to the Basement," which they in turn had lifted from Bowie. Pedaling straight 8s on the root note of the chord. Hold down, say, the A on the fret and thrum it *dum-dum-dum-dum-dum-dum-dum-dum*. Now you're Sid!

You didn't need a record company, you didn't need to know how to play your guitar. This was the whole idea behind Punk: Do it yourself. D.I.Y. Consciously disdaining musicianship was at the heart of it, and Sid was the living proof of rock's D.I.Y. credo. The *ur*-myth of rock had always been that anyone can play, but previous to Punk this remained a figure of speech. It did not literally mean *anyone*, it meant anyone who could play an instrument. But Punks weren't going to settle for an approximation like this, a smarmy euphemism. No! They would democratize rock, radicalize what had heretofore been a disingenuous bromide by taking the myth seriously.

The Flowers of Romance rehearsed in a squat in Shepherd's Bush in the autumn of 1976 with Sid on vocals, Keith Levene, Steve Walsh, Albertine, and Palm Olive on drums.

"When I first met him he was quite polite," says Viv Albertine. "I'd heard a lot about him, a friend of John's: they looked like bookends, the pair of them with their spiky hair. I was expecting spiky hair but when he got there he'd shaved his head, looked hideous. . . . I always felt uncomfortable with him: he was so strict, and so idealistic and so clever. That is what people don't realize: Sid was so sharp. . . . He was

55

so quick: that's why he had to look thick, to slow himself down."

Leee Black Childers described the Flowers of Romance as a combination of the Ramones and the Sex Pistols. "They played Ramones, couldn't keep time. Very much the one-two-three-four! syndrome." Sid started out as a singer and went on to playing the sax! These were people who could hardly play but were interesting enough to get interviewed a lot. Sid wrote some of the songs, with titles like "Brains on Vacation," and "Piece of Garbage." *"Kamikaze pilots / Want to die / Frederick's of Hollywood / Husband and I." "Yer as bad as TV!"* And, of course, the infamous "Belsen Was a Gas."

Sid may have been the living incarnation of D.I.Y. but he was dedicated. He practiced. Yeah, he did. He had a surprisingly strong sense of purpose and commitment, actually sacking Viv Albertine from the Flowers of Romance because she couldn't *play*.

Sid, the embryonic rock-star-as-fan posing in front of the mirror. An accomplished clotheshorse like Sid had it down cold. Alright then, pose number 1: I'll do a line of sulfate and learn the songs later. The great Keef Richards 'imself said, "I got the moves down first, learned to play later." Awright! A-one-two-three, "Ain't no cure for the summertime blues." *Yeah!*

Run intercortical news-file footage of the netherworlds of London Punk—fast-moving cinema verité clips. You, Dante in spandex circa 1976, enter the crepuscular realm of garish, unhinged characters! Disturbing images! Lydon and the lads taking acid at Louise's—an exclusive lesbian club on

Poland Street in tony Mayfair. Chrissie Hynde in a corner writing letters for *Penthouse Forum* on wet napkins.

The Sex Pistols had their sharpened magic together. All the elements in place—drop-dead style (courtesy of Westwood and McLaren—and now Lydon), slogans (McLaren and Jamie Reid), aesthetic propaganda (Reid), rhetoric (Rotten), sound (Messrs. Cook, Jones, and Matlock), flaying lyric assault (Rotten). This seamless integration of style and sound wasn't always the case with the bands that followed in the Sex Pistols' wake. The Vibrators, for instance, seemed like promising contenders but they lacked the moral content of the Sex Pistols. The Damned lacked the musical coherence—they even played the occasional Beatles song, fer chrissakes. But with the Sex Pistols all the elements came together and played off each other—and in the process generated a particularly rabid species of fan.

Sid conformed almost uncannily to the personality profile of the rock fan/rock star compiled by the Greater London Metropolitan Constabulary. They have identified fifteen stages in the etiology of the rock fan/rock star thing: Fan at home, listens pathologically to radio, waiting for his song, *the* song to come on . . . becomes obsessed with lead singer . . . buys star's records—*all* his records . . . begins slavishly imitating mannerisms of idol . . . goes to concerts, hounds star . . . gets into clothes, aggro . . . incipient megalomania . . . identifies totally with rock star—he *is* him . . . morphs into embryonic rocker . . . moves off in the mirror, air guitar . . . the decisive moment—buys guitar . . . joins/forms a band . . .

involvement with drugs . . . becomes famous . . . kills self (see suicide–accidental death variants list) . . . fan at home listening fanatically to the radio, etcetera.

Like a schizophrenic in his solipsistic cave, Sid hallucinated many strange and disturbing things. The most ingenious—and fully developed—of his fantasies was that he had telekinetically summoned up the Sex Pistols out of the *prima materia*, the oceanic *umwelt* of adol-essence. Of the Sex Pistols' album, he said: "I wrote all the songs." Said it in all seriousness. What on earth could he have meant? You *know* what he meant: "I am he who creates what he identifies with because they are all me. They wrote those songs using *my* persona." He believed this.

I am clearly their number one fan an they bettah bloody know it! I didn't know 'ow to dance so I jumped up an down an bashed into people, the consequence of which bein that me epiphany, so to speak, occurred on a Tuesday, the eleventh of May, 1976. 'Ere was I at a Sex Pistols venue an filled wif the parousia of the 'oly spirit I starts jumpin up an down wif unfettered exhilaration—actually I done it so as to see the silly buggers play by leapin up to peer over the 'eads of them in front of me. An blow me down if I do not inadvertantly invent the pogo an by the which obtain immortality. Or wot little one may procure in this vale of tears.

Here was the archetypal fan, the Punk zealot incarnate, Sid Vicious, the Sex Pistols' number one fan. Enter the fitful head of Sid. Compulsive thoughts—like suras in the

Koran. Not a theory or an analysis of the thing, but the flame of belief itself. Martyrs have died for less.

It's a metaworld. Once in the teen substream you live continuously in the daydream, a meticulously constructed fantasy that is impervious to outside assault—parents, teachers, bosses, authoritarian busybodies in general. Why should you pay homage to the tired old *designated* reality? You are part of something huge, something that will change the world. You—Sid, Siouxsie, Viv Albertine—you're part of something that only you and a few friends know about, a coven. You know the Big Secret Thing.

> WIFOUT MESELF—THEIR BIGGEST FUCKED-UP FAN—ALONG WIF SIOUXSIE, JORDAN, SUE CATWOMAN, AND THE LOT, I ASK YOU, WHERE WOULD THEY BE? FINK ABAWT IT. INNIT THE VERY FERVOR OF US VILE FANS AND ALL THAT HAS MADE THE SEX PISTOLS WHAT THEY IS TODAY? LET'S FACE IT, WE IS THE SEX PISTOLS FUCKIN RAY-ZEN-DEBT. WE IS THEM AND THEY IS US AND WE ARE ALL TOGETHER. . . . FUCK, I'M STARTIN TO SOUND LIKE THE BLOODY BEATLES.

The Sex Pistols were all about breaking down the barrier between audience and performer. Baiting the audience was integral to their code. At first it was all very democratic and open—the space between performer and fan a white-hot center where everything melts, the two elements mutating into each other. It was central to Punk's program to demystify, deglamorize the band, defuse the star state. It's a short step to believing the two elements really are one. An illusion that Punk in general and the Sex Pistols in particular encouraged. The hive thinks, "It's our group mind as has directed them."

Whenever the Sex Pistols didn't blast through—even *they* had off nights—their storm troopers could be counted on to stir things up. Punk violence was at first theatrical, McLaren and Westwood inciting acts of violence at the Nashville or at the 100 Club.

Beating up randomly selected members of the audience on a slow night made for good theater. Little riots made all the Punk costuming and posturing seem more authentic. At this point, at the beginning, it was really just Method acting. If the show needed a dose of "spontaneity," a bit of the old ultraviolence goosed it. Part of the spectacle. The scene was well overamped on amphetamine sulfate, anyway.

"People just wanted to go mad," said Paul Cook. "We were the catalyst."

But the line between theatrical violence and real violence early on became blurred. Especially when you're dealing with borderline cases like Sid. Violence was catnip to Sid. When Vivienne Westwood slapped a girl's face at the Sex Pistols' second show at the Nashville (the set was dragging), you can see Sid actually licking his lips in Kate Simon's photo.

Gobbing, pogoing, safety pins, studs, leathers—the look depended on the implied violence, and real violence was just a boot away.

Suddenly the audience is interacting. Alarmingly. Like Sid and his mother, they were children of liberal parents turning against their parents. Against decorum, against acceptable social behavior. And what could be more of an affront to Brit propriety than smashing someone in the face for no particular reason. Just because you bloody well felt like it.

At a Clash concert on the twenty-third of October, Shane MacGowan bit off the ear of fellow fan Jane Crockford. Mutilation fantasies. Sid involved in the melee. He'd also been involved in the violent incidents at the Nashville and the 100 Club. After a while Sid conveniently forgot the name he'd been given was a joke. Led around by the nose, by his own name.

Sid, like Punk itself, was testing the limits. But since rock is not the real world, the lines weren't where they should be. Anything was acceptable. And who's creatin' the big kerfuffle? Wadin' in there wif the bicycle chain. It's *'im*—Sid.

Jimmy McCulloch to Sid at the Speakeasy: "Pity you can't play the bass, Sid." Sid smashes a bottle and shoves it in his face. That'll show the cheeky bugger who can play!

"I don't like your trousers," says Sid to rock writer Nick Kent and takes out a bike chain. *Wack!* Blood all over the place, and right away Wobble the old speed-freak jumps in and has a go at him, too.

This violence business was volatile philosophically as well. McLaren and Westwood were as slithery as eels on the subject. Their position could change on a whim and overnight you could get moved from one side of the T-shirt to the other. The night of the trousers/bicycle chain incident with Sid, you've got Vivienne Westwood apologizing to Nick Kent, explaining that Sid's a psychopath, he'll never be at one of our concerts again, and a week later calling Kent a little weed. And Nick had once been a Sex Pistol! Well, for a week or two—early days.

In the middle of a Damned set, during their spin-cycle version of the Stooges' "1970," Sid supposedly throws a beer glass at the stage, it smashes on a pillar cutting several people, and a glass splinter hits a girl in the eye, blinding her.

This incident lands Sid in the Ashford Remand Centre. He writes a letter. "I get so agitated in here that I can't sleep at all. When I do I get the most awful nightmares. I'm reading that book about Charles Manson, which Vivienne lent me, and I'm finding it quite fascinating." Lighter reading material next time round. The lesson gathered from this experience is not the one intended: "One of the things I believe in since being slung in here is total personal freedom." Be *more* extreme.

Sex Pistols fans were like a newly evolved species tuned in to the frequency of the alpha mutants. Signals went out— beaming *thisisitthiisitthiisit*—and the Knowing Ones, antennae twitching, sensed the pulse, tuned in to the beam. In the middle of the day—hennaing their hair, watching telly, buying a packet of rubbers—they'd walk out the door, get on the tube. The call had gone out.

They start out on their crusade with a tiny fanatical group of the elect. Thirteen people in the audience, club the size of your average living room, a stage four feet deep, umbrella strobes.

Sex Pistol fans are fanatical. Since nobody outside themselves and a handful of others has ever heard of the Sex Pistols, it is a cult thing. Just friends of the band, which by a sort of pop mitosis doubles and triples each time they appear.

I am rudely awakened by Jonesy pourin a bottle of wine on me face. "Wake up, you wanker, we is going out for more rapin an pillagin." 'Ee knows me weaknesses, that boy. I gird up me loins an out into the night.

And 'oo does we run into at the Speakeasy Club but Bob Arris, a baldy ol' sheila 'oo does a pathetic program the name of which—the Old Grey Whistle Stop—sez everyfing.

'Ee's in a jolly ol' gin-fizz mood an the first fing 'ee sez, all poncey like, is: "If you lads play your cards right I might"—emphasis on the might—"have you do a turn on my show."

"Fuck awf!" sez I. To which he rejoins: "You're nothing but a mob of uncouth jobs. I think nothing of you at all." All very lah-de-dah he goes.

"And you," quoth I, "is just a ol' cunt."

At which point he comes all red of the face an flustery like I'd said somewot that 'ee did not comprehend.

"How dare you!" sez 'ee like an old tart from a BBC wankers-of-the-ages series.

"I fink I'll slit the tosser's gullet straightaway if no one objects," sez I, all stroppy. Clearly a jest, but the ol' fart is a right drama queen an begins squealin like a stuck Northumbrishire sow. "Oh my god," 'ee declaims, "someone help me, they're trying to kill me! Call a constable!"

One fing I will not stand for is shabby melodrama. We depart forthwif. Next day our contract wif A&M is cancelled.

Mary Harron: "There was something electrifying about the mythology the Sex Pistols had brought with them. They were chaotic, it was wild. . . . In England, there was a nightmare coming to life, it was overpowering and disturbing. Something had been given permission to show itself, it was exploding out."

Rotten was becoming something of a comic-book character. Already, star morphology was decomposing the remnants of Lydon. Like his hated anti-self, Mick Jagger, Lydon had the ability to spin an image around himself, multiply himself in screaming, mewling, puking, gobbing phlegm, mimicking hunchback poses.

The Pistols were a magnetic center around which all the haywire energy spun. They were saying, "We don't give a fuck!" Saying, "Move over!" to the Who, the Stones. They'd found the crack in the wall. Once breached they would stream through into their self-created future.

Not everybody got it. In Hull, there was mass incomprehension. The audience became nasty, incensed by the Sex Pistols' professional ineptness, *the same fucking song fifteen times over!* Everything about the Sex Pistols outraged them. Their appearance, for one. They were a bloody joke, wasted good money on them, we did. But these people were anachronisms. Hopeless. And whom were they expecting, Peter Frampton?

In Hull, even the groundlings missed the point. But then, they lacked the right equipment. This was not the insect colony with twitching antennae tuning in to the electron god. They, the infidels, had confused the mystic hum of ecstatic rage for *mere noise*. Good. Better! The Sex Pistols' signals were impenetrable to even your seasoned rock audience. Within months they were infamous. Cancellations escalated. Good. Better! The fine-tuning must be working.

'Ee's getting increasinly inward, Lydon is. I'm worried about 'im, I'm tellin ya. Gettin weird an sarcastic, or else 'ee's wiffdrawin. An the uvvers always complainin abawt they don't get their names in the paper. But wot the fuck they expect with names Cook an Jones? Get yourself a fuckin flashy name like Rotten an me! Got meself a violent, cartoony name. Problem is livin up to the little bugger. Unlike the uvvers, 'owever, I am prepared to go all the way.

12

Electricity Comes from Other Planets (The Genesis of the Pistols)

> In the beginning there was boredom . . . the gods were bored. Then they created man. Afterwards, Adam was bored, so Eve was given to him. Adam and Eve, Cain and Abel grew bored en famille; then humanity en masse; and when the Tower of Babel was built, boredom overspread the earth in layers as thick as the tower was high.
>
> —SOREN KIERKEGAARD, *Either/Or*

IN THE END, IT DIDN'T TAKE MUCH FOR MCLAREN TO SET THE Sex Pistols rolling down the track. The timing was perfect. Insularity, conformity, respectability, stifling officialdom, had created a suffocating climate. A depressed economy . . . the craving for novelty . . . the long-awaited decline of the West . . . the tabloid press's need for a bolshy bogeyman . . . the angsty *sitzfleisch* of music critics . . . whatever it was, by 1976 the ideal conditions existed for the arrival of the Next Big Thing. In mid-seventies England everyone, and not just your wayward youth, was disenchanted.

Quality of life was rapidly deteriorating; the country was mummifying. Malign portents began showing up: two-headed calves, circles in the wheat. Things were getting out of control on a large scale. A full-fledged capitalist recession was under way (7 percent unemployed), the government toppling, currency devalued, living standards plunging, decaying inner cities, poverty. Not to mention the politeness quotient plummeting, social life more dismal than usual, and the grey old things in Whitehall still dithering on in dusty rooms. No wonder the country was cracking up.

Everything was going to hell in a handbasket. But this distressing state of affairs wasn't going to culminate in a fiery apocalypse—nothing like that. That at least would have been something of a change. The world in flames! Just like the Blitz!

But this! It was all happening at such a *dreary* pace. Not with a bang but a whimper. Sterility, cynicism, boredom. Theoretically, class and race and gender were gone. Bland. We were all the same. This hadn't, of course, happened in England. It never will, but the pretense was there. Everything leveled off, everything the same only worse.

Since the early seventies, the decadence of the Weimar Republic as portrayed in *Cabaret* and *The Damned* had become a common metaphor for Britain's decline. And now Punk. Just the thing to dramatize England's 19th nervous breakdown. It was the theme music of collapse.

The Intercity to Birmingham forty minutes late, bus strikes, tube strikes, bad food, bad sex, bad faith and other domestic indignities. People began to long for unreasonable remedies. An absolute horror of boredom—*anything* but that!—was developing in the land.

Polite little islands like England and Japan have a need

for periodic splurges of pandemonium. Order creates boredom and boredom breeds monsters. Punk fit the bill perfectly.

The conditions were ripe for tremors in the field. Boredom being the very thing to bring on the future. *New and improved* cheap thrills were needed. We were at the end of a long-declining empire, the illustrious past now mere pageantry. More than anybody, the insect trust, the rock fans with probosci drooling in anticipation, were ready for the new food of the gods.

Out in the provinces where *really* nothing happened, they had scanned the horizon for any signs of life. *For years.* T. Rex, Mott the Hoople, Roxy Music, Hawkwind—these were talismanic names, groups that seemed to have the key. But nothing was coming through.

Exhausted from rampagin an feelin a mite catatonic from the massive infusions of spirits, I lays meself down on the proverbial corporate couch. Very comfortable it is, too. I commend 'Erb Alpert an Mr. M. on their taste in furnishins. Abawt to go forty winks when one of them A&M dollies comes in an requests as I kindly remove me foot from the sofa as I is drippin somefin' vile on the upholstery. But wot the fuckin 'ell is this? Me bleedin foot is bleedin somefin wicked an all you care abawt, you cunt, is the fuckin chintzy couch?

Lydon 'as gutted a armchair, anuvver of our company frews up in a ashtray. Secretaries gaze on in 'orror at the scene of devestation we have wrought. I address the little whores wif me usual politesse: "Me foot's bleedin. Can you find me a fuckin plaster, you bitch?" Which,

oddly, receives no response wotevver. Right! If you will not minister to me grievous wounds I will 'ave to nurse it meself. An so toddle off to the loo to bathe me wounded foot in the porcelain fountain of Bethesda. So there I is, sploshin me afflicted foot in the cool waters of Battersea an soothin me frayed nerves. But, misfortune, alas, pursues me even unto the bog.

While steadyin' meself wif me elbow, it inadvertently goes through the bleedin window an as a consequence of said dislocation I slips on the floor an breaks the fuckin toilet bowl. Jesus wept! Could 'appen to anyone, now, couldn't it? At which point a coupla tossers in Afghan coats rush in pretendin to come to me succor but in actuality to tut-tut. "You all right, man?" they arsk. "A'-course I'm not bleedin awright, you stupid cunts, wot you fink?" Their beady little all-mod-cons eyes alight on the broken glass an shattered bowl an a great lamentation goes up. You'd 'ave thought I'd smashed the fuckin Venus de Milo or somefin by the sound of it.

'Avin demolished the offices of A&M records we bid them adieu, an a sorry lot we is. Cook wif blackened eye an bloody nose, me wifout me shoes drippin precious bodily fluids all over the Saxony plush wall-to-wall, all the while me an Jonesy stuffin our pockets wif loose bottles of booze until we looks like the Michelin Tire man.

Our naughtiness is duly reported back to the high muck-a-mucks at A&M, who wif great 'igh dudgeon makin noises all: "Oh, dear, what have we wrought?" I'll tell ya wot you 'ave wrought, old darlins, you 'ave just signed up Attila the bloody Hun an 'is merry men.

At length we hie ourselves back to our doss in Denmark Street where all collapse on Fatty's bed. By an by TV news pops in to shoot a little at-'ome-wif-the-Sex-Pistols interlude. Very bright lights is switched on. Momentarily awake all groggy like but wif me usual aplomb I issue a statement to the press to wit: "I 'ave 'ad the greatest time o' me life, old sons. This is me first day an as far as I is concerned it is great bein in the Sex Pistols," quoth I like Princess Margaret greetin the natives in Pogo Pogo an then out like a light I go. Wot timin, lads!

13

The Boy in the Box

WHAT DID THE HIVE WANT? COLLECTIVE BUZZ. LITTLE FLECKS of desire, angst, boredom, forming an image.

John Lydon had not been chosen as randomly as McLaren would like us to believe. More in the manner of the Dalai Lama. He had all the signs: the charismatic aura, the dandy's narcissism, the canny look of the holy tramp who's wise to it all. *Pied Piper will lead you to the water.* Bin liners, safety pins, berets, granddad pants—whatever. A veritable Punk prophet. He even had the oracular stare of the possessed, the look of one who has seen too much. A metaphor for the hypnotic power of vision, of genius (or of madness commonly associated with genius).

Rotten was the archetypal Punk-as-fop, a reverse fop if you will, but a fop nevertheless. A dandy who not only lives in front of a mirror, but is himself a kind of mirror, showing others their reflections. A Gorgon's glare, paralyzing the audience. A stunned look that parodies the voyeuristic stare of the fan. Caused by meningitis (he tells us) but this is clearly more a case of iconology than etiology.

> **We're here, time tourists wif the Spirit of Fings Gone Awry as our guide. Let us then partake of a peek in the window of 430 King's Road. Look, there's our dear old shopkeep, Malcolm McLaren, and seamstress Vivienne. And 'oo's that lad, his face pressed against the shop window? Tell me, Spirit. Know you not wot 'ee is, child? That's is John Lydon, soon to be known to the world as Johnny Rotten on account of 'is rottin teef.**

Lydon, a dandy to the manner born, had his own idiosyncratic sense of style. He took the old vagabond look and burlesqued it with a constellation of safety pins, badges, and patches, topping the whole ensemble off with—a nice touch!—spiky green hair. Green hair was not entirely new to rock. But in previous generations it hadn't been exactly *intentional*. Your old rockers (and the glam crowd, too, of course) loved to dye their hair blond. It was the pink Cadillac look. The extraterrestrial rockabilly singer with the Porter Wagoner frozen-custard-wave front. But not realizing the expressions "bleached blonde" and "peroxide blonde" are something of a metaphor, many a wannabe blond rocker had poured a bottle of peroxide on his head only to discover that their hair had turned bright green the next time they shampooed. Perhaps Lydon had seen examples of this. Or maybe it was just the Irish in him.

Lydon-Rotten was a Finsbury Park Rimbaud. An almost flawless reincarnation (circa 1976) of the *poète maudit*. The vagabondage, the flashes of temperament, the surreal lyrics, the hostility, the *look*. It was as if Rimbaud's ghost had flown out of the Abyssinian desert and incubated a bozo kid from Finsbury Park.

> STEVE JONES: I thought he looked pretty and I said to Malcolm to look out for this bloke. That green hair, and that. And he'd come in the shop and then Malcolm must have asked him: "Do you want to sing?" and he said, "Yes, I don't mind." Or something. We was all piss taking. We thought he was a bit of a bowser, and like he was really flash. He put Alice Cooper's "Eighteen" on the jukebox.
>
> PAUL COOK: We thought, He's got what we want. Bit of a lunatic. A front man. And we knew straightaway. Even though he couldn't sing.
>
> GLEN MATLOCK: They just thought he was kind of a puppet character. A bit nutty. A bit kind of psychotic. And he stares good, you know, he's got a good stare. So he embodied the whole thing. He's got the right face.

A cool narcissist exhibiting a hard, reflecting surface. Detached, self-contained. He disdains displays of emotion and affects a well-honed indifference: *"There's no point in asking, you'll get no reply."*

When McLaren saw this, saw John Lydon dancing in front of the jukebox at Sex, he knew he was the one:

"He really couldn't sing, he had no sense of rhythm, but he had this charm of a boy in pain, trying to pretend he's cool.

That was the most accessible thing. You knew all the girls were going to love him."

Here, then, was the mudlark that he would make into a star. Lydon, reborn as Johnny Rotten, was the Punk Everyman in an almost Paul Bunyan–ish sense of the word. In one way Lydon *was* anybody—couldn't sing, couldn't even keep time, etcetera—but for that very reason he was the Punk kid incarnate. Just as, a year and a half later, Sid would be a nobody taken to hallucinatory intensity.

With characteristic whimsy, McLaren elects John Lydon lead singer of the Sex Pistols. This is McLaren's experiment number 1. Take a boy off the street—virtually any boy with a bit of your Cockney impudence and an overdeveloped sense of flash—no prior experience (or talent) necessary, and within six months make him a star. Unfortunately for Malcolm, into his well-laid plans came two very potent nobodies indeed. And in succession.

John Lydon, *mutatis mutandis*, was Malcolm McLaren. It was as if McLaren had wished him into existence. They were the spitting image of each other, physically, psychologically. The popping eyes, the narcissism, gift of the gab, indifference to public opinion. Both Aquarians. For McLaren's purposes Lydon was himself as he might have been—and yet not.

McLaren liked to flirt with chaos but in Johnny Rotten he was dealing with psychic material far more combustible than he was used to with Cook, Jones, and Matlock. Lydon saw the setup for what it was: "They wanted me to be this mystery figure they could hide in the cupboard and spring out like a jack-in-the-box. Close the lid when it's not needed anymore." Not bloody likely.

Once Lydon injected himself into the Sex Pistols, the symmetry changed utterly. In place of accommodation, compromise, balance, resignation, even, there was now disruption, angst, radical instability. Lydon had his own agenda: the Sex Pistols as a means with which to vent his guilt and anger.

With the infusion of Lydon's petulance and narcissism, the Sex Pistols became what the Bay City Rollers pretended to be: a teenage band. The Bay City Rollers were a record company's idea of a teenage band. Bubblegum rock. The Sex Pistols were the real thing charged with sullen, snarling, angsty confusion.

Lydon inverted the dynamics of the group. He had to. They'd got it all wrong. It wasn't about a good ol' rave-up, it was about taking all that working-class aggro and *using* it. Lydon wasn't having any of Matlock's rock 'n' roll pantomimes: "Glen wanted us to be a camp version of the Bay City Rollers. I'm sorry, I was completely the other way. I saw the Sex Pistols as something completely guilt-ridden." He needn't have worried. It was a miasma of suspicion and mutual incomprehension from the start.

As a figurehead for the Sex Pistols you couldn't have found a better, a more elusive spokesman than Johnny Rotten. Irony and sarcasm were his stock-in-trade. You never knew where you were with him. Even his mum was nonplussed: "He's a funny boy, always talking in opposites." His ability to change his mind—as often as his outfit—was phenomenal. In that little chapbook of Punk aphorisms, *Johnny Rotten in His Own Words*, you can find any number of ex cathedra statements contradicted on the same page. Sometimes in the same sentence: "I'm a worm, I'm god."

Lydon as Johnny Rotten had enough of Bowie in him to keep everything in suspense. But where Bowie was the Great Oz, pulling strings behind a scrim, Rotten was a serial enigma. His multiphrenia wasn't just a series of poses but an actual *point of view.* The Punk P.O.V.—everything at once. Nothing if not postmodernist. With Lydon—and this can hardly be said of Bowie—you clearly sensed, behind the chameleon posturing, a ferocious core personality.

If the members of the Sex Pistols didn't get on—so much the better. "Cultivated hatred is your greatest asset," was a McLaren dictum. Cook and Jones never really cared for Glen, and Glen seems to have barely tolerated *them.* He also detested the abusive Rotten when he arrived on the scene. Rotten, in turn, had nothing but contempt for Glen. Cook and Jones never much liked Rotten, nor he them, and it went on from there. This tangled mass of hostility would act as a differential engine within the band. It would be their means of propulsion. "I think it was the animosities between us," says Lydon, "that made the songs what they were. . . . We didn't add any bridges. We were very good at burning them, though."

The aggravation escalated as the Sex Pistols' fame spread. Put the tension into the music, the performance. It's that churning, unsettling element in the Sex Pistols that gives their sound its feral howl. That made them mesmerizing to watch. It's not what they say or play, so much as the twisted way it comes out—all that hostility seething around the words.

> "Cook an Jones," quoth I, "where'd you get them names, outta a Christmas cracker? You'll not prosper wif names like that, old son. Cook an Jones is, as you should know, the names of haberdashers, butchers, bakers an candlestickmakers. Too fuckin mundane an tedious, an that ain't the half of it. My suggestion is you try somefin wif a bit of élan, such as Montmerency and Winterbotham. Then at least you can pose as a coupla pooftah antique dealers when you retires from the game."

Cultivated aggro is a Brit thing. A concept often confusing to Americans—even fellow Punks had a hard time grasping it. When Legs McNeil, the resident mascot at *Punk* magazine, finally met the Sex Pistols backstage at Winterland, he was confused, disenchanted. Here was the most notorious band in the world, *the* Punk band and they "didn't seem to be having any fun."

There's the difference right there between Bowery punk and U.K. Punk. Your Yank is a pleasure seeker. It's written into the Constitution. He sees the snarling coven before him and deems the Sex Pistols pathological for their failure to enjoy themselves. It's true, they were at their lowest point here—going to split up in about five minutes. But you have only to look at pictures of them on the Swedish tour or in Paris to see it's never far away, the tension is always there smoldering. Gloom, friction, hostility. Cook giving the two-fingered salute while Rotten is sitting off by himself under a perpetual black cloud like some Punk Hamlet.

And while all this stress was amping up the internal engine of the band, Malcolm was out there hustling. McLaren modeled his strategy on Andrew Loog Oldham's blitzkrieg tactics, manipulation of the press and bald-faced fabrication. Oldham had achieved his sleight of hand through an uncanny ability to lead the press by the nose. He fed them their lines—"The Rolling Stones are the group parents love to hate," and "Would you let your daughter/sister go out with a Rolling Stone?"

Of course, Oldham had the best possible material to work with. It's doubtful whether he could have promoted any random group to such a pop apotheosis. But intuition is also a key component in the impresario's bag of tricks. The divining rod of the true Svengali will identify the chosen

> PARTY ON, DUDE.
> SOD AWF!

ones. The Stones would have emerged at the top of the heap anyway, but part of an astute manager's self-image is to conjure the illusion that he alone is the source of all wonders. For all his trashing of the Stones as boring old farts, they were clearly McLaren's idea of a pop New Model Army and his strategy with the Sex Pistols—as had been Oldham's with the Stones—was to jump to the head of the parade and make them the standard-bearers of a generation.

Even the weather was on their side.

14

Sun, Sex, Sulfate, and Swastikas

THE SUMMER OF 1976. THE HOTTEST HEAT WAVE IN ENGLAND since 1940. Punks running wild through the crumbling capital. London, as in a J. G. Ballard novel, briefly becoming equatorial. The middle class could escape into their air-conditioned flats, offices, banks. The streets, "like some magic beach," were now the playground of the historically dispossessed. As if all the Marginals—teens, blacks, gays— were inhabitants of a Third World country that had sprouted up spontaneously within the U.K.

Hot weather made the atmosphere hallucinatory, it escalated the fantasy—or had the overcharged, overamped sensibilities of Punk, like a synergic flash fire charged the air itself?

Cue Julien Temple footage:

The sun sets at Marble Arch and so you get that incredible shaft of light, a very epic feeling. I remember Sue Catwoman walking in a see-thru raincoat, backlit in the sunlight down this Victorian Street. They were like a Velcro ball rolling down a slope.

The suppurating brain of a decaying empire. Hot house plants growing freakish mutations in the humid *rotting* climate. Degeneration! Enervation! The country's at its pathetic nadir and along come a bunch of kinky moronic yobs and jump on its head. Like extras in some post-apocalyptic bomb movie, young boys dressed as bums, derelicts, alcoholics, old moth-eaten men with fantastic stories, shoes without socks, Dickensian urchins on the prowl. Girls dressed like whores from hell. Cybercunts flashing their pussy in broad daylight. Insinuating truly degrading acts of humiliation. Bondage! Masochism! Lick my boots, toilet slave.

All this! And fueled by the teen drug of choice: speed. Leapers were the propellant as they had been for the mods. Side effects: irritability, suspicion, restlessness, overexcitement. Serious mental disorders, delusions, schizophrenia, grandiosity, hostility, and aggression. Read the label! A perfect chemical cocktail for the existential leap into the pluperfect present.

The summer heated up by pent-up frustration fused onto no-work, no-future, on-the-dole malaise. The thin, nasty veneer of Brit respectability stripped away by a social demonology as acerbic as paint remover. The decay of the old social orders was almost *visible,* giving off a putrescent glow. Walking through London you could see horrible sights. Proleptic Punks—Luddites, *Clockwork Orange* malchicks in boiler suits—climbing out of their coffins in London's summer of the living dead. Chunks of misplaced schizophrenia flying through the air. Eaten alive by squirming psychic maggots.

The Sex Pistols came to power in the crepuscular light of the last gasp of sixties hedonism. Twilight's last gleaming, just before the Thatcher *reich* closed in. It was the sixties bomb party all over again, except this time round it was all done in black light, the actors in drag. Swinging London had been a fiction wished into being by any number of young people. The Punk apocalypse was more *Mad Max.*

July 1977. Swedish Tour wif dear ol' Boogie. Huge bloody crowds. Last night they wouldn't let us out the stage doors, those fat cunts. They said the crowds would tear us apart, but nuffin 'appened. I won't be filled wif that superstar shit. I absolutely despise those turds. The Stones should 'ave quit in 1965.

Everybody is gettin fuckin exhausted an all. Squire Rotten broodin off by 'issel finkin dark medieval fings that 'ee does not divulge. They is all fuckin basket cases—except for meself a'course. I am becomin the veritable nucleus, the bloke 'oo keeps the spark alive on account of I am a great one for bein a personality. Wifout exaggeration I would say I am carryin all the charisma on me own back wif this bunch of geezers.

Stockholm Airport and 'oo does I spy wif my little eye but me fave raves of all time, ABBA. Completely pissed outta me mind I rushes up to 'em, an almost grovelin like, sticks me hand out so they might grace it wif their signatures. An wot do they do, the ingates? Scream an run away. Thought they was bein attacked, the silly bitches. 'Aven't they ever seen a hand wif pus oozin outta it before?

15

The Movement

All this was gloopy and made me smeck, but it was like nice to go on knowing one was making the news all the time, O my brothers. Every day there was something about Modern Youth, but the best veshch they ever had in the old gazetta was by some starry pop in a doggy collar who said that in his considered opinion and he was govoreeting as a man of Bog IT WAS THE DEVIL THAT WAS ABROAD and was like ferreting his way like into young innocent flesh, and it was the adult world that could take the responsibility for this with their wars and bombs and nonesense. So that was all right. So he knew what he talked of, being a Godman. So we young innocent malchicks could take no blame. Right right right.

—Anthony Burgess, *A Clockwork Orange*

Like all pop movements Punk started with an elite. But there always comes a point when the elect lose control, and mass market and mass media take over. This is how something *becomes* pop. A necessary modulation, but along with the transition everything changes. As fans far removed from the center became involved with the Sex Pistols, a fresh burst of energy was released, with unpredictable results. Nuance and irony were the first things to go. Ambivalence, mock deviance, paradoxical posing, faux fascism—all those shunting equivocal postures—you can kiss them good-bye right off the bat.

Thanks to McLaren's propaganda and Rotten's weekly

bulletins, Punk seemed to have a coherent philosophy. The first pop movement with yer actual theoretical underpinnings! Go on, ask him anything. John Lydon Esquire, on the Queen, religion, Freddie Mercury, sex, the dole, symbolist poetry, people who stand in line. . . .

Plus the U.K. itself is a sort of pop megalab. Unlike the U.S.A. or most other Eurostates, in England the media, the gossip vines, and the fashion industry are very centralized. It all goes down in London—newspapers, radio, TV, fashion, gossip, pop music. You go to sleep with the Same Old Thing and the next morning you wake up and the Next Big Thing is everywhere. On the telly. In every rag, on every hoarding. Full-blown, like Jack's beanstalk. In this respect the U.K. is the ideal pop kingdom, a toy principality where vague notions can become national issues, and fashions catch on instantly. It's also—or was until very recently—a monoculture, which makes it the just place for testing out new trends. The whole country is one giant boutique.

As soon as the Sex Pistols poked their heads above ground they became national bêtes noires—something that might take years in the U.S.A. Notoriety overnight! Too good to be true! As sources of outrage they were perfect, providing a convenient pretext for the always-welcome moral crusades of the "We've got to put our foot down" variety. Ideal bogeymen for the tabloid press. They more than adequately fulfilled the requisite horror-movie image of hooligan teenage gangs on the rampage: green hair, dog collars, vinyl T-shirts, nazi insignia. Look, dear, some fresh monsters with your bangers and toast!

It was as if some fiend had made a list of all the things

your average Brit feared and found repulsive and had given them life.

This they had to put up with! The shawbaties of the Empire were turning on them, their children morphed into hideous mutants and threatening them in broad daylight. You couldn't walk down the High Street without seeing these geeks vaunting spiked purple hair, orange mohawks, bare-boobed bints in see-thru bin liners. This was the menacing horde of bolshy youth out of one's worst nightmares. This was what they'd been anticipating all along. Perhaps their own paranoia had summoned up these hell-spawned changelings. Hair-raising stuff.

Really just teenagers parading; suburban kids dressing up. To give it any more weight than that would be like going to a see a play, and when the assassin comes onstage the audience rushes screaming from the theater. As absurd as that. But the tabloids, of course, are in the absurdity *business*. Outrage sells papers. Readers love to feel that frisson, the sense, when you open your paper, that the world is going to bloody hell.

The tabloid press is a Ptolemaic universe: there is nothing new under the sun. Everything that comes along is reduced to its crudest state. Manichean good and evil in furious battle on a darkling plain. Either a *good* thing (not too newsworthy) or AN ABOMINATION!!! In 60-point type.

Rule number 1: Always deal in clichés. Irony doesn't translate to the tabloids. Rock 'n' roll, however, is by its nature ambivalent. Obfuscation being one of the principle objectives of a cult. Its signals are *designed* to be impenetrable by outsiders, adults in general being the classic case of the excluded. Plus you have to take into account that teenagers aren't quite sure what they're talking about anyway.

> Nice to read abawt yourself in the papers now an again, innit? Gives one a feelin of existential substantiality, know wot I mean? Viz: review in *Sounds* by one Jon Savage— I'd very much like to inquire where 'ee procured that name. Scribed the little Savage: "Vicious, legs astride playing adequately, but he looks the part." Very perceptive, that. An all you uvver bloody critics can sod awf! So I play one riff, wot of it? I is a specialist in that regard.

In the eyes of the Punklings the scandal sheets are nothing more than consortiums of adults in their most doltish state. They, the bungling hacks of the tabloids, are *meant* to miss the point. They can always be counted on to misinterpret signals—especially those involving any level of ambiguity.

Never mind the irony, here's the filthy, pervy Sex Pistols. Fleet Street couldn't distinguish the threatening theater of Punk from the reality even if they wanted to. To them, everything is literal. Besides, they had a vested interest misreading Punk's extreme manifestations.

It's traditional with them. The Stones' Redlands bust in February 1967 being a prime example. How could a bunch of rock musicians on an acid trip ever be interpreted as a serious threat to British society? Hysteria is barely subcutaneous in the U.K. There's always an epidemic of social demonology waiting to erupt—and carefully incubated as an ostrich egg in the tabloid press. Consequently no youth culture is real by the time you read about it. Teens in places far away from the cult's core read the misinterpretations of the press and further misinterpret them.

When the *Evening Standard* comes out with an article about a "new apocalyptic cult with a harsh dogmatic attitude," you know you are right on target.

As the Sex Pistols caravan began moving down the road, the metaworlds of the press, publicity, and rumor were out there multiplying levels of reality.

Any shred of subtlety that was left after the tabloids had chewed through the Sex Pistols was reduced to farce within the first twenty seconds of Thames Television's *Today*, presented by one Bill Grundy. Sarcasm, mutual loathing followed by baiting and then on to mild obscenities.

GRUNDY: What was that rude word?

LYDON (schoolboy voice): Shit.

GRUNDY: Was it really? God, you frighten me to death.

LYDON: Oh, all right Siegfried.

The nasties begin when the silly old prat tries to chat up the pert, cheeky (and blonde) Siouxsie along the lines of, "I'll see you after the show, dearie." Steve Jones won't have any of this.

JONES: You dirty old sod. You dirty old man.

GRUNDY: Well, keep going chief, keep going. Go on, you've got another ten seconds. Say something outrageous.

JONES: You dirty bastard.

GRUNDY: Go on again.

JONES: You dirty fucker!

GRUNDY: What a clever boy!

JONES: You fucking rotter!

You could say that this hardly seems like the seeds of a national scandal. But you would be wrong. Thames Television switchboards are jammed with protests from angry viewers. Lorry driver James Holmes, forty-seven, is so incensed he kicks in his TV set. For swearing on telly, a vanload of police are called in. Headlines in all the papers next morning. When asked about the incident the bristly Grundy says, "You can fuck off!"

> THE DAY AFTA THE GRUNDY SHOW— "THE DAY THE AIR TURNED BLUE"— THIS WAS IN ME OPINION YOUR ACTUAL BEGINNIN FROM THE MEDIA POINT OF VIEW OF PUNK ROCK. THE TABLOIDS DIDN'T 'ARF WORK THE GENERAL PUBLIC UP ON THIS ONE INTO A RIGHT FRENZY.

Soon the Sex Pistols are banned everywhere. You'd have thought Attila the Hun and his Mongol horde were coming down the M1. These outbreaks of moral indignation play beautifully into the hands of McLaren and the band. Almost overnight the Sex Pistols have acquired a quite unearned reputation as bad lads. Their infrequent appearances (due to cancellations by nervous local boards) bestow on them a mythical aura.

Jamie Reid: "The media was our helper and our lover and that in effect was the Sex Pistols success, as today to control the media is to have power of government, God, or both."

And . . . the naughtiness continues. . . . Run footage of the Sex Pistols on pop-music show *So It Goes*. Slagging off Clive James, as "a terrible Australian straighty." Look! There's Jordan calling him "a baldy old sheila." The shock of incomprehension. On both sides. Egad!—Wot's this? Don't tell me there are still groups in matching blue Dacron suits. How is this possible in the year of our Lord, 1976? Wait, maybe it's camp. No, but it clearly isn't. Clueless bloody stooges. A band called the Gentlemen (how'd they ever think of a name like that?) slope on saying their favorite singer is Joni bloody Mitchell. Oooh, wot bloody weeds!

The press working themselves up into a fine froth—ah, it's time for Malcolm to make his move. With the seven songs the Sex Pistols recorded during July 1976 in Denmark Street, he now has something to hustle. The Black Prince of Pop going head-to-head with EMI and Polydor, and the fuddy-duddy British record industry lumbering along trying to catch the vibe.

They're in the biz of domesticating lightning, basically. Unpredictability doesn't appeal to them. They want a smooth-running organization, the old dears, and rock has become a fairly routine business by this point. In comes a new batch of likely mates with their demo, and the record company bloke is saying, "What you got for us, lads, then? Country, pub, or progressive rock? Country with a dash of reggae, is it? That's a nice twist. Let's have a listen." All conceivable avenues of rock have been explored, mined, excavated and refined. There are *categories*. The categories have long been established and, with the exception of a few oddities—Bowie, Roxy Music—there isn't anything that couldn't be labeled under one sticker or another. The only question is where do you fit in?

The Sex Pistols don't fit in, which would have been bad luck for Malcolm had it not been for the press very conveniently foaming at the mouth. Thanks to the tabloids the Sex Pistols are now a *phenomenon*, and a phenomenon sells itself, it's prepackaged.

On the eighth of October McLaren signs a contract with EMI for 40,000 pounds. Pretty astonishing for a group that started out barely a year ago as a near-hopeless bunch of Swankers and wankers. McLaren's ego and ambition now inflate exponentially. Such unrestrained hubris adds a further sting to the roiling pit of vipers.

Having launched the Sex Pistols, McLaren is on to *"Next!"* He thinks he's sussed how the popzeit functions—the media-generated buzz that accumulates around bands, brands, and fashions—and he intends to work this vein with a vengeance. On to the next scam! Then people will know the Sex Pistols are just a bunch of nobodies, that without McLaren they would have been nothing. But then again, there was Sid.

Me first press conference—at the poncey Regents Palace Hotel. May I say I acquitted meself brilliantly. (I fink.) May 'ave inadvertently imbibed a bit too much vodka but wot is it there for if not to get drunk on?

Regrettable but necessary mash-up wif Paul. The altercation begin over the seminal question—a bloody obvious proposition if you arsk me—as to oo is the most Sex Pistol. Not meanin to do 'im an injury but in the process I bash in 'is nose. The silly bugger will not listen to reason so wot's 'ee expect? No 'ard feelings, is there, eh Cookie? Hold on there a tick, those is me only fuckin pair of shoes. Bugger! Out the bleedin window. Air-mailed me bloomin shoes down the area.

16

The Toy That Exploded

FEBRUARY 1977. TENSIONS WITHIN THE GROUP REACHING CRITical mass. You couldn't really blame them. It's all going too smoothly. Making everybody bloody nervous, it is.

"We're not into music, actually. We're into chaos," is their line. Chaos is a touchy commodity; it has to be coddled. Once it gets on the telly, gets its mug in the paper, it's in danger of going soft. Don't want to end up like the Dave Clark Five, do we? Buying a one-up, one-down with all mod cons in Petts Wood. Not to worry, though. With Lydon as commissar of pique there's always plenty of free-floating abuse. The animosity is focused on Glen Matlock. Boot out the smoothy.

Rotten's list of grievances: "Glen was a mummy's boy. The best musician out of the lot of us, but too bogged down in the Beatles." And, added Malcolm, "He acted like a squirm."

There's worse: His hair and clothes had got really neat. He was lettin' the side down, the smarmy sod! Further: He was indulging in harmonies. *Harmonies!* 'Oo does 'e bloody fink 'e is—Paul McCartney? Unwanted, old son, to say the fuckin' least. Next charge: His playing on the demos in January was too *funky*. Veering dangerously in the direction of hippie get-down sessions. How many times did we tell ya, ya wanker: mon-o-lith-ic. Wall of noise is what we're after. Then there was the ol' reverse snobbism going against him. Glen came from the wrong side of the tracks—too middle-class, hah hah. Oh, and one more thing: He was chubby. Sorry mate. Bad for the image, that. We gotta look hungry and angry. The sans culottes of the council houses is what we is going for.

It's John who gets rid of Glen. Insists Sid replace him. "Sid was John's protégé in the group," says Julien Temple. "The other two just thought he was crazy."

Matlock had been the glue; gave their sound a structure over which the chaos could rage. Still, he was an emblem of that vile disorder: competence. As far as Rotten was concerned it was too much like the old musos club wanking off on their scales. It was making him nervous: "We were getting too good. We needed Sid."

The myth of the Sex Pistols' incompetence has been greatly exaggerated. Still, it's a wee bit of an embellishment to say Glen got booted out just because he was too professional. Sid was needed for other reasons. The Sex Pistols were in danger of becoming a smoothly running pop band. For the Pistols Mach III, more outrage was needed.

Sid was Punk in its purest form. DO YOUR OWN THING! ALL POWER TO YOUR-SELF! THE RAWER THE BETTER. Sid would take the *farce* seriously, take it to its illogical conclusion. Congratulations! You have won the lottery to be in the world's most hostile rock 'n' roll band. Self-destruction being part and parcel of the pack-

WE DO THE SIGNIN IN FRONT OF BUCKINGHAM PALACE. THAT'S ME, FAR LEFT, AS IF YOU COULDN'T TELL. AN MIND, JUST THE FACT THAT I'M 'ERE INSTEAD OF GLEN MAKES A HUGE DIFFERENCE. ALL FEATHER DUSTERS AROUND 'IM WAS GLEN, MUM'S GOLDEN BOY. AN WOULDN'T YOU KNOW IT, WIF HIS SEVERANCE PAY GLEN 'AS GOT 'IMSELF A SUNBEAM ALPINE. BRILLIANT.

age. They chose Sid to act out the final phase, where they're sucked into the abyss, the *malebolge*, Dante's eighth circle of hell.

But Sid would take it all to another level. Where Rotten played the mad artist, Sid *was* the willful, violent child.

Cinderella Sid. He'd gone to bed John Ritchie and woken up Sid Vicious. Sid the Incubus visiting him in the night, taking him over. His newly hatched doppelgänger had little irony about itself. Like most doppelgängers, it was going to swallow him whole.

The Sex Pistol virus went directly into his bloodstream. On February 13, 1977, he performed his first duty as a Sex Pistol and came through with flying colors: a sarcastic phone interview with a Los Angeles deejay. Brilliant!

FEBRUARY 13. I become a Sex Pistol. Well, one fing, wif me in the band the 'ole enterprise is got more on a serious metaphysical plane. Me own personal theory of wot makes the Sex Pistols the fearful quartet that we are is: confusion. No one can bloody understand the fuckin fing, includin ourselves. Wot they cannot comprehend in this country they attacks—that's the U.K. for you. The police, the teds, the government choose to smash us down at every opportunity. Today John got nicked between the sandwich shop an the studio. Traces of amphetamine sulfate in 'is jacket linin. An 'ow many times I told the silly bugger to snort his pockets out? A filfy 'abit it may be, but it is a prudent observance when residin in a fascist regime like as we got 'ere.

17

Becoming Sid

SID! PROTO-SID. JOHN SIMON RITCHIE, TALL, GOOFY, CHARIS-matic. There's a fragility to him, a giddiness. Nervous, fear-ful, like the pet hamster for which he was named. He was without roots or the anchor of family. Brittle teenage identity. Peter Pan on drugs. As his mum Anne Beverley said: "The best thing you could do for him on a Saturday would be to buy him a water pistol—at seventeen and a half. He loved toys. He could fire those guns at the cat all afternoon."

Where they came from. Ask Lydon to describe it for you. "Picture this: Dead-end ladies leaning out of the win-dows with their hair up in curlers. Beans on toast with fried eggs. The works. The Victorian slum dwelling. It's now illegal in Britain to rent out buildings like that."

And what was he like, then, Sid—er, Simon? Ask his mum:

> He was a natural musician almost from the day he was born. When he was eight months old the thing he liked to hold was his da's [John Ritchie] trombone mouthpiece. At two years old he was out in the garden singing, "That old black magic has got me in its spell" with all the inflections, the lot. He'd drum away for hours, with the saucepan and two sticks.

Lydon and Sid were both very close to their mums. Jon Savage described Sid's relationship with his mother as "more like conspirators than parent and child." Leaves home at fifteen. Comes back. At seventeen, after a row (repeated a million times a day around the world), she tells him: "Simon it's either you or me and it's not going to be me, so you can just fuck off."

About the same time, Lydon's dad tells him to cut his hair. He does—then dyes it green. Gets thrown out of the house and begins squatting with Sid in Hampstead in the abandoned buildings in the back of the station. They are officially desperate people. They can now do whatever they want to. The shy, cerebral Lydon and Sid, the acter-out. Stubbing cigarettes out on the back of their hands. One of the games they played.

"He loved the art classes," says Anne Beverley. "But he

quit after the second term 'cause they tried to make him do particular subjects. It turned him off. He was always the person who could not be told what to do. He had to do his own thing. I always lost all the arguments."

Doesn't want to work—angry images of claustrophobia. council flats, dead-end jobs. Sod that! He tries prostitution. The creature of modern industrial society, the orphan with his gun. The Hammer horror-movie look. Disgust. Registration of unidentified horrors. The Burroughsian Wild Boy with the unsettling animus of the gang member. Preternatural coolness. The male impersonator's ambivalence.

He's a shameless groupie with the addled fan's delusions of intimacy with stars. Forever tracking down the likes of Bryan Ferry and plotting to bring round a bottle of Martini & Rossi vermouth, have a cocktail and a chat. "Let us lift our glasses to the workin' classes!" Lydon is too proud (and too shy) for such exhibitions. Still, it's this curious side to Sid that led indirectly to Lydon becoming lead singer for the Sex Pistols. Sid's the first of his crowd to go into Sex, introduce himself to McLaren, and bring along Lydon, Wobble, and the rest.

And it might just as well (at least according to his mum) have been Sid as Lydon who turned up at Sex that afternoon and became the lead singer of the Sex Pistols: "Simon was working in the Portobello Road market that day. Now, that should have been Simon and he was really pipped at that, really put out."

"[Sid] was a Punk way before Malcolm came on the scene," says his mum. "Right from '75 when he first dyed his hair, he was Punk. He carried it all the way through. . . . Sid knew Malcolm was selfish and careless and he loved him for it."

Sid is in many ways Lydon's opposite. Humorous where Lydon is dour; physical, violent where Lydon is cerebral; literal where Lydon is ironic. Both poseurs in the final analysis. Cook knew it the moment he saw Sid: "Another arty-school type," he said to himself, "like that fucking wanker Rotten. It became a circus. Sid was up John's alley. He was the same type of guy. That cocky art student with a smart-ass attitude. Here we go again, not another one. I could deal with John, and now there was two of him."

They were birds of a feather. Inseparable. "Sid was my mate. Great! Another one out of the slums. Success here. . . . I wanted Sid in the band because then I would have an ally in all of this. Sid couldn't play? So what. Anyone can learn. I learned to sing, didn't I? He wasn't too bad at all for three-chord songs. It was a bass guitar, for god's sake. Who listens to the bass guitar in a rock 'n' roll band? It's just some kind of boom noise in the background."

They'd met at Hackney Technical College, each as he was emerging from the fog of childhood.

Lydon:

He was a Bowie fan. He'd do silly things to get his hair to stick up because it never occurred to him to use hairspray. He'd lie upside down with his head in an oven. Sid was such a poseur, a clotheshound of the worst kind. Whatever the new style was he'd have it. . . . He was a soul boy when I first met him. You know the uniform. It could be midwinter and snowing and he wouldn't wear a jacket. He had naiveté which is a good quality, a kind of innocence, but he lost that. He couldn't see dishonesty in people. He was funny, he would laugh at everything all the time. Everything would be the ultimate amusement to him. Life as a joke.

Sid remembers Lydon around this time as "a balding old hippie

SITTIN ROUND DENMARK STREET DAY AFTA FUCKIN DAY WIF LYDON ALL MOODY AND SILENT AS A EEL AN THAT. PEOPLE GOING "WOT RHYMES WIF 'ON THE DOLE?' "

" HOW BOUT 'STUFF IT IN YER HOLE?' "

COOK AN JONESY DOIN HIS CAPTAIN BEEFHEART IMITATIONS. WIF TALENT LIKE THIS—THESE GUYS ARE ALMOST PROFESSIONAL THIEFS—YOU'D FINK THEY COULD AT LEAST STEAL A FEW BLOODY RIFFS. USELESS BLOODY SODS.

wif a big pair of platforms on. That's wot you were."

Sid and Johnny were both obsessed with style but at opposite ends of the spectrum. Lydon was a dandy, he invented fashions of his own devising. Sid, like a fashion-mad hermit crab, went from one style to another until he found the perfect fit, shamelessly trying on the latest fad. Bowie clone, soul boy, glam. Sid cared what people thought of him, hence his fixation with clothes. Sid needed the identity that style would give him.

Lydon names him—did it 'ave to be after 'is foul-lookin albino hamster?—and, hard as it may be to believe, Sid was, at first, mortified when given the most notorious name in all rock.

I hate the name Sid, it's a right poxy name, it's really vile. I stayed in for about two weeks because everyone kept calling me Sid, but they just wouldn't stop. Rotten started. He's 'orrible like that, he's always pickin' on me.

Lydon not only names him, he hips him to Punk couture and the Richard Hell bog-brush hairdo. Now the thing from the netherworld is ready to go. He is on. In his ripped, swastika-covered T-shirt, studded wristband, and spiky coif bracelet, he is an instant celebrity.

Sid had the look. Looking the way we *should* look after a century of horrors. Fright, electrocution, mutation, mutilation, zombie-assassin, tormentor–tormented, demon–damned, victim-perpetrator, Nazi-Jew, sadist-masochist—all fused together by nuclear blast.

A Gary Panter cartoon playing bass. His leather jacket bristling with studs like the spines of a poisonous strain of feral boar. Homicidal psycho replicant with lairy gaze like a wild, rabid dog. Not a Saturday-morning cartoon like Joey Ramone, but something menacing—like *Spawn*.

18

The Quest for Eddie

(The Square Root of Rock)

THE FIRST TEN SECONDS PHYSICISTS CAN NEVER ACCOUNT FOR in the creation of the universe. That blinding center from which all else emerged as if from the cosmic fireball. But the center was missing. Where was that elementary particle of the sullen, anguished teen soul that flew out of the dark void of banality and created all things? Not just rock music, but the birth of coolness itself. Attitude, babe. An existential dread and nausea so potent as to make Sartre puke.

There was the alien from Tupelo, of course. Elvis may serve for the average person's messiah of rock but he was anathema to Punk. The embodiment of compromise, self-indulgence—the befuddled, manipulated, flabby rock star. A travesty of his own gospel. Maudlin, kitsch, bloated. He was a gullible redneck and—like Sid—easily led by the nose.

For most forms of expression—music, art, architecture—this lack of origin might prove problematic, but rock is without history. It exists in an everlasting present. The radio, the CD player, tape, MTV video clip, all exist—once rolling—in the real time of rock. The perpetual howling Now. Rock—somewhat like sex and drugs—has no past.

True, there are outmoded genres in rock but they are aberrations and, in any case, when they cease to be part of the canon they fall into the dreaded realm in which dwell such cheesy items as "Up, Up and Away" and Partridge Family theme songs.

There used to be an honorable home for old rock songs: the Oldies But Goodies category (to which fifties rock 'n' roll has now been permanently consigned); but today no viable post-fifties rock 'n' roll sound ever becomes an "oldie," it becomes classic rock. Hey, lissen, there's classical *music*, isn't there? Do they call Mozart an "oldie but goodie"? It would be offensive, would it not, to refer to Messrs. Led Zeppelin, The Who, the Rolling Stones, or Hendrix as "oldies but goodies"?

Still, every generation gets to create its own family tree. Brit bands are especially adept at drawing up rock genealogies. The Stones had created a line of succession for themselves which began in the mists of Central Africa, continued on up Highway 61 to Robert Johnson, Muddy Waters, Howlin' Wolf, Slim Harpo, Bo Diddley, Chuck Berry, Otis Redding, Smokey Robinson, James Brown—all culminating with *them*. A variation on the standard Brit blues canon. And while it contained novelty songs (signs of eccentric genius) it disdained most purely pop music, even Elvis.

SATURDAY, APRIL 16. In 'orspital wif hepatitis. St. Anne's Tottenham. Wot 'as transpired is the followin: after playin Screen on the Green slid off ta score some Chinese rocks wif Keef. Consequence: I turn yellow as a Chinaman. I is deafly ill. But do any o' those cunts come to visit me? Nah! Worse fings to come. No one must have any knowledge wotsoever of me dire affliction. Me perilous condition 'as to be kept a deep dark secret because, accordin to that twit Malcolm, the Sex Pistols—I kid you not—do not take drugs. Fuck awf, sunshine! 'Ee must be goin bloody barmy, silly ol' prat! But let's face it, the Duke of Deviance is a puritan at 'eart, like all reformers. 'Ee is amazed at all the in-out an the ingestion of synthamesc an uvver controlled substances that goes on regularly in the bog at these gigs. Malcolm 'as a prudish disdain for the sexual deviations an fetishism 'ee exploits through 'is work. Wot a pervy ol' tosser!

Consequence of which nobody visits me at all or even knows I am alive (sniff). If it weren't for Nancy upon whom I 'ave come to rely indubitably I would go crackers.

Bein in 'orspital affords ample time for reflection. In me rare moments of lucidity I 'ave to own up that Sid and me is not entirely commensurate wif each uvver. By the which I mean to say the bugger is nuffin like me whatsoever.

Rock 'n' roll may have begun with R&B, but for Punk the mythical origin of rock in the blues wouldn't do. The blues was too gris-gris, mojo-laden, too black. Blues, the engine of sixties rock, had been co-opted by hippies and was therefore by definition out of the question. Besides, locating the origin of rock in the blues implies nostalgia, a compromising sentimentality that would emasculate the drive of urban albino aggro rock.

R&B undeniably had that steamroller sound, but that elemental, earthy, funkiness was itself a stumbling block. It was perfect. You couldn't really do it *better* than Howlin' Wolf, Muddy Waters, Buddy Guy and Junior Wells. Anyway, the Stones and the Yardbirds had already gone down that road.

You had these weedy, little Brit boys hollering, *"I'm a man, spelled M-A-N"* and that shit, moaning about collard greens and grits, and juju hands and other stuff they'd never seen. Pathetic. Pretending to themselves that Hackney was somewhere off Highway 61.

When Howlin' Wolf played in the U.K., he couldn't, due to the arcane bylaws of the Musicians Union, bring his own band with him so he picked up sidemen. Little Brit blues gnomes. These boys all knew his repertoire backwards. But the sight of this Mount Fuji of the blues—six-four, three hundred fifty pounds—in the throes of constant eruption, primal rage radiating from him as buckets of sweat poured down his face, and there at his feet—these *tiny* English boys—it was hilarious. Lilliputians! Elves, in tailored jackets and Anello and David boots, who seemed to come from another planet. Rock had to hightail it out of the Delta on the next Greyhound bus.

And then there was this *other* problem with big daddy R&B. It may have been sung by bad-ass black dudes, gun-toting black muthafuckas, mojo conjure women, but they were *adults*. There was an irony, a wry, world-weary take to the blues that was entirely incongruous for the melodramatic teen sensibility.

The closest historical antecedents to Punk attitude in fifties rock were perennial Brit rocker idols Eddie Cochran and Gene Vincent. At South London rock swap-meets, Gene Vincent's leathers were frequently displayed and treated by teds and Rockers with the reverence usually reserved for the foreskin of Christ. They'd become sexually excited in the presence—trembling, sweating, finally breaking out into a bit of the random ultraviolence. But Vincent (with his gammy leg and weight problem) had blown it.

Eddie Cochran had come as close as anybody to the sought-after existential ferocity of 1950s rock. He was clearly the Sex Pistols' (and Sid's) favorite. But by no stretch of the imagination could you say he'd invented rock 'n' roll. He was part of the second wave. And as for the requisite self-destruction bit, does getting killed in a taxicab in Chippenham, Wiltshire, really count?

What to do? The Punk solution, their way around this was, characteristically enough, straight out of science fiction. Not that difficult a feat since Punk saw itself as the Alpha and Omega of Rock anyway. Punk was the origin that *should* have been. Now, *at last*, the culmination of rock history. After us . . . nothing!

Okay, so the mystic moment when the teen pantacrator conceived of rock didn't exist—so what?—you had to create it.

To hell with history! The diamond sutra of rock (and blues and jazz) wasn't to be found in its origins but in its refinement. Wasn't the essential menace and ecstasy of the blues to be found not in the Delta but in Chicago blues? The apotheosis of jazz not in its New Orleans roots but in bebop? Ergo, if all immortal rock resided in a continuum, one didn't need to locate the missing square root of rock in the *past*, one could simply *create* the cosmogonic origin myth

> **MIKE PETERS SEZ THAT "THE IM- PACT OF THE PISTOLS IS NOT THEIR MESSAGE [WOT MESSAGE? ED.] BUT THAT PEOPLE CAN ALMOST SEE RIGHT THROUGH THEM AN STILL FIND SOME- THING THERE." FIRST SENSIBLE FING I'VE READ IN AGES. AN AWRIGHT GEEZER.**

oneself. Anytime. What did it matter if it was out of chronological order? In the eschatology of Punk the end was the beginning, anyway. What mattered was the Holy Wail. The thread was lost, hidden, and only the pure in heart would find it. A red dog with exploding eyeballs comin' at'cha out of the time tunnel.

But how to deal with the inconvenient lacunae of rock history? Chop it and channel it. Take what you want and chuck the rest. It's like a lost conversation picked up near one of the moons of Jupiter. Re-forge it, Jim lad, in the smithy of the present! Parody will do quite well, thank you. As a matter of fact, put-on is the best way of dealing with this stuff without contaminating yourself. The Talking Heads' take on Al Green's "Take Me to the River."

By the mid-sixties, twitching teen antennae had located

the frequencies that most closely matched their own. Teen proboscises dipping into the soundstream—Brit beat groups, rockabilly, Eddie Cochran, garage bands—extracting their synthamesc essence. A process of refining, winnowing. Noise and urge, raging lust, in-your-face aggro, the X factor. Hysteria, imp of the goof, wipe-out, gonzo. Elements that didn't fit this criterion—fatback drumming, earth-shaker bass, and all manner of funk in general—were discarded. Until the black elements in rock were progressively bleached out.

Punks assembled a demolition derby of sound. Flashy, stripped down, high-octane wheels. Cocky, strutting, belligerent, sullen. Like arachnids siphoning off the most noxious strain from the carcass of rock, they extracted the thin shrill whine of a cranked-up, overamped machine, a metallic scream like the sound of burning liquid hydrogen. Like a 747 taking off. *That* noise.

It's a fruitless business looking for the origins of the Sex Pistols in the Ramones, in the New York Dolls. It's like saying Mort Sahl was Lenny Bruce's *predecessor.* Which is why the so-called precursors of Punk are such a fucking joke. *As if we owe them anything. Sod off!*

19

Muse on Horse

Enter Nancy. Within days of Sid's joining the Sex Pistols, Nancy Spungen arrived from New York. Richard Hell's description of her is one of the more charitable:

> She was a fairly typical suburban girl who worshiped rock stars, she had an exceptionally large drive to be where the action was. . . . Nancy just wanted to be somebody (not necessarily herself) and you've got to hand it to her, she made it. She would do absolutely everything to get what she wanted.

You may trash her all you like but what is Nancy but the Saint Teresa of Punk? Like a sacred whore of Babylon, her life was entirely in the service of the true faith. Just like Sid. A true believer.

> **NANCY GETTIN INTO LYDON'S FACE AN 'EE IS POISED TO SMACK 'ER ONE. "OH, DON'T HIT HER," QUOTH I, "YOU MUSTN'T." NANCE AN ME IS INSEPARABLE. TOGEVVER WE STAND, TOGEVVER WE NOD AWF.**

Nancy had come to London in search of Jerry Nolan from the Heartbreakers. She couldn't find him and ended up at Louise's gay bar in Mayfair, and then Linda Ashby's tony S&M establishment where she met John and Sid. She first tried to pull John, and when that didn't work, ended up with Sid. Just like in *Sid and Nancy*. Run the clip.

20

The Pistols Aesthetic

"Maybe though," says Vivienne, "Brenda doesn't have the foggiest idea of what's going on, the old burke. In that case, I'd feel sorry for her. I compare her to those people in the Polynesian Islands who are taken away at a very early age, kept in a dark room, and stuffed with food. Then they bring them out once a week so everybody can revel and marvel at these very pale, fat people who can't walk, but have to be helped along a sort of catwalk."

May 27, 1977. Sex Pistols release "God Save the Queen." Bashing barre chords. It was a hit record, by the way. Moving into a rhythm pattern similar to "Anarchy." And then there's "Pretty Vacant," from their 1977 LP, *Never Mind the*

Bollocks, Here's the Sex Pistols. Opens with a muted single-note riff repeated many times, moving into a basic chord progression using mostly 1 position chords. "God Save the Queen" opens with slid-into bashing barre chords—similar to the Misfits' "Who Killed Marilyn"—and then moves into a rhythm pattern similar to the one they used on "Anarchy."

'ELLO, IT'S 'ER MAJESTY'S SILVER JUBILEE! CUE "HER MAJESTY'S A VERY NICE GIRL." MALCOLM IS IN A LATHER RACKIN HIS BRAINS AS TO WOT TO GET HER——THE WOMAN AS HAS EVERYFING. 'EE'S GOT A PERFECTLY VILE PLAN WHICH I CANNOT IMMEDIATELY DIVULGE. MUST GET OVER TO SEX, 'AVE A LISTEN IN ON VIVIENNE'S INTERVIEW, A RANT ON THE QUEEN, BASICALLY, WHOM SHE REFERS TO AS "BRENDA."

Lyrics sawed off, blunted, filed down. A series of insults held together by the logic that holds insults together: rage. "Satisfaction" with its faux existential grope is positively ethnographic in comparison to the lyrics of "Submission": *"I can't tell you what I found/Submission/Submission . . . Going down down/under the sea/I wanna drown drown/under the water."*

When Lydon sings *"I loooove you"* in "Submission" it's a joke, a parody. The misogyny in "Satellite" is rancid. Comparing this girl, Shanne Hasler, to a big, fat baked bean! My word! A new low in rock misogyny!

Jonathan Richman's "Roadrunner," which the Sex Pistols played in rehearsal, one of the first songs they learned, is close to Bad Company, heavy rock with pop overtones.

Unlike, say, the Dead Kennedys' one-minute blitz, "Nazi Punks Fuck Off." Like hearing the Sex Pistols on 78. Goes by so fast you can hardly decipher the words.

Speed and intensity are the essence of Punk. The Sex Pistols produced your basic three-minute songs.

Paul Cook:

Our songs aren't fast. Most people think about Punk songs being three-minute thrashers. I would try and hold everybody back a bit, especially Steve. He liked to go full-steam-ahead without thinking too much about it. . . . Everyone was so pumped up . . . I would slow the band down. Relax, let's not go too mad.

"Anarchy in the U.K." is essentially a pop song. It isn't a barrage of noise, it's an actual tune that lodges in your head. The Sex Pistols were working within a strict format. Their songs for the most part carefully constructed. Not that much different from what Suzi Quatro was doing, or the Sweet's "Teenage Rampage." Soundwise they're very put-together; the *Bollocks* album outstrips any other Punk album of that period.

The Sex Pistols, as much as they'd like to deny it, were very much tied in to a pop sensibility. Despite all the bluster about how aggressively unmusical and untogether they were, they came up with a bunch of hooky, chorusy little three-minute riffs. Not all that unlike ABBA—one of Glen Matlock's favorite bands.

England's stasis, patriotic decay, was furiously fetishized in Punk songs. Nineteen eighty-four was going to be the Punk Jubilee. Bring on lives of noisy desperation! Postmodern children of Dickens with their theatricalized poverty. They could give a toss. They'd just as soon smash it—*Awf wif their fuckin' poncey heads!*—put the stake through its rotten royal heart. The anti-monarchical railings of the Sex Pistols summoned up the demons of time. Cromwell. The English Revolution (1649–60), a strange, surreal time when people were excited beyond all expectation. Julien Temple compared Punks to the Cromwell period. Moral fervor—just like the Sex Pistols. Johnny Rotten was a latter-day ranter himself, like Abiezer Coppe's (circa 1646) inspired ballad "The World Turned Upside Down."

> THE MYSTICAL POWER OF THE MONARCHY. ANY MUCKIN' ABAWT WIF 'ER MAJESTY WILL RESULT IN HARSH RETALIATION. MEANWHILE DOWN AT THE PUB 'EE'S SAYIN, "YOU KNOW THE BLOKE THAT BROKE INTO BUCKINGHAM PALACE? THEY RECKON 'EE DIDDLED HER 'IGHNESS WHILE IN THERE AND THEY HUSHED THE WHOLE THING UP. GOT IT FROM A SPECIAL FORCES OFFICER AT THE TRACK." CHEERS! HERE'S TO ENGLAND'S NERVOUS BREAKDOWN!

Loss of position in the world put Britain in a psychotic state, and U.K. groups with their bohemian arty milieu knew how to push the buttons. Imagery from *The Texas Chainsaw*

Massacre and *Pink Flamingos*. A fix from porno magazines. Amputees, bondage, Charlie Manson, anything taboo. Total cultural revolt. They even got the old peanut planter worked up. Jimmy Carter began saying he wanted to stop Punk. Ah, just mix yourself another mint julep, Jimmy, and slip *Eat a Peach* on the turntable.

> **JUNE 7, 1977. Queen Elizabeth II Silver Bloody Jubilee as queen of Great Britain, Northern Ireland, an all the uvver little wankers great an small. Bloody buntin' an bonfires all over the place. Souvenir industry gone completely mad, wif coronation mugs an coronation scarves an coronation bras an God knows wot uvver rubbish. But to me mind this is no more than coverin up a disintegratin mess wif fadin coronation wallpaper. A million fuckin idiots go down to 'ave a look at the procession from Buckin'ham Palace to St. Paul's Cathedral. Bollocks! Wot, standin there in the heat all day just to catch a glimpse of the old burke trundlin past in 'er glass slipper?**

Releasing "God Save the Queen" in time for the Queen's Jubilee—a complete coincidence, I assure you—was bad enough, but Malcolm had to pour salt into the wound by hiring a boat on the Thames called the *Queen Elizabeth* so he could put up a huge banner which said all in caps: QUEEN ELIZABETH WELCOMES SEX PISTOLS.

They do "Anarchy in the U.K." going past the Houses of Parliament and "God Save the Queen" going past the Tower of London. Fuckin' great! There's a scuffle on the boat. A minor skirmish involving a photographer but—out of the blue!—police are boarding the vessel. Giving rise to the excellent *bon mot:* "I didn't know pigs could swim."

Retribution comes swiftly and terribly. Soon after, Jamie Reid, Sex Pistols propagandist and designer, gets his leg and nose broken by patriotic morons. What did he expect, when you stick a safety pin through the Queen's mouth? The following Sunday John is attacked in the car park of the Pegasus pub by a gang of knife-wielding thugs. Two tendons in his hand severed, a machete-chop cut right through his leather trousers. *Oi, wot's a machete doin' in fuckin' Highbury, then?*

Malcolm's disinformation machine has so confused the press that the *Sun* has to ask "Was it all a publicity stunt?" *Confusin' innit?*

Next you've got PUNISH THE PUNKS!—all-caps headline in the *Sunday Mirror.*

Following "God Save the Queen," a slow retreat, a long decline for the Sex Pistols—and the Queen. This was their high point. Shortly afterward things start coming apart. McLaren has a momentary inspiration: "Wouldn't it be great to just disappear? Just be a hit-and-run?" *Wot a bleedin' genius!*

After "God Save the Queen," the Sex Pistols are a pop group with a number one record (despite being banned). By the summer, they are careening into overexposure in the U.K. By the end of the year, the Sex Pistols are on the cover of the *Investors Review* as "Young Businessmen of the Year."

Rotten, already paranoid, blasted out on speed, is living with Wobble, Gray, Nancy, and Sid in the Chelsea Cloisters. Now that alone would drive you barmy, wouldn't it? With Rotten, paranoia has become a perfectly acceptable social state. A suitable state of mind for the end-of-the-world scenario. Paranoia as a metaphor . . . hmm . . . for what? For exacerbated religious fanaticism, onanism, inversion. Zealotry of the raving, gnostic type? I suss rampant neo-medievalism at work here. Expect battles between angels and demons, virgins and whores. The Temptation of Saint Rotten! Considers hisself victim of a conspiracy of demonic powers (including the government), extravagant persecution by "society." Lydon is fast becoming the pseudo-Areopogite of King's Road. Fuckin' 'ell, this is wot 'appens when you run outta sulfate in the middle of the bloody night. Perhaps such a circumstance as this brought on the Middle Ages proper. Wot *did* they use to get outta their heads, anyways?

PLAY ME FARTY OL' BASS PART ON "GOD SAVE THE QUEEN" AN "BODIES" BUT THE LADS SEEMED TO LIKE IT WELL ENOUGH. PROBABLY ERASED THE LOT AS SOON AS ME BACK'S TURNED. GLEN, THE BLOODY WEED, WOULDN'T EVEN PERFORM "GOD SAVE THE QUEEN." HE THOUGHT IT WAS SACRILEGIOUS, SEE? WELL, A 'COURSE IT'S SACRILEGIOUS, YA BURKE, THAT'S THE BLOODY POINT, INNIT?

Needless to say, all this aggro is making Rotten bolshy. Turning up at a photo session dressed as a teddy boy—where's his Punk gear, then? asks the irate McLaren. When asked to select his fave raves on that poncey pop-radio show, he sez: "Neil Young, Peter Hamill, Dr. Al Imentado, and Captain Beefheart are me main influences." *Wot??* "I like *all* sorts of music," opines the wily Lydon lad. McLaren meanwhile is spinnin' in his swivel chair. " He's doin' it to get me goat, the little fuckah!" That's right, Malcolm.

Meanwhile Sid is slowly unraveling. Frankenstein's monster threatening to run out of control. No gigs, shut in with Nancy, Sid is rapidly becoming uncontrollable. In early December, the pair make the front page of the *Sun* for smashing up a hotel room. Sid feels himself in an impossible situation. He is the newest member of a group that he once thought were the best in the world and which is now so inactive that he isn't sure whether they (or he) exist.

Malcolm tries to get rid of Nancy by putting her on a plane with a one-way ticket back to the States. But she is too terrified to get on the plane without drugs. The whole thing just pushes Sid and Nancy closer together, and in Sid's brain plants a hatred of McLaren, which he will never shake.

Masses of highly public hostility come down on the head of John Lydon. Johnny always did have a mission to change the world, silly bugger. Playing the gymnasium at Brunel University in Uxbridge, the Sex Pistols are confused by the size of it. "This is horrible, it shouldn't be like this. I'd seen us as a small clubby band. We were way ahead of ourselves. We didn't know how to get past the first twenty rows," says Lydon. It is a fiasco.

Tension grows between McLaren's continuing need to manipulate and take credit for the Sex Pistols, and the band—with Rotten at the helm and Sid friggin' in the riggin'—sailing on, according to its own lights. An ongoing disaster-about-to-happen.

By August, Punk is really coming on. Nineteen seventy-seven is the second year of Brit Punk. The Clash, Siouxsie and the Banshees, with whom Sid Vicious first played bass, the Stranglers, and Generation X with Billy Idol. *My aim is true!* Elvis Costello's first album comes out.

The Pistols have been together barely six months and already books are being written about them, two movies (*The Great Rock 'n' Roll Swindle, Who Killed Bambi?*) are in the works (both of which liberally mix fact and fiction). Sid always hated films because "people have to act parts in them." Well this was even spookier. Here he had to play himself.

Who Killed Bambi? Wif Russ *Beyond the Valley of the Dolls* Meyer involved, there's bound to be lots of dollies wif big tits an all. They've cooked up a right poxy movie, Malcolm an them. The usual bollocks, teenagers tryin to overthrow the establishment. Marianne Faithfull plays me mum. We shoot up together an have a violent, incestuous relationship. Lovely. Replete wif a lead villian named M.J.—a obvious euphemism for Mick Wotsisname—'oo, after revivin 'is career by impersonatin Johnny Rotten, is killed as the Sex Pistols crash the party that celebrates 'is comeback, afta which punks take over the world. Yeah, right! But a enchantin sentiment, nevertheless.

Just as well *Who Killed Bambi?* never got made. Rock 'n' roll movies are a doomed genre. They undercut the inter-cortical movie that involuntarily rolls in your head whenever the song plays. An infinitely adaptable script. You, Writer-Director of Earthly movies Sponsored & Angeled in your own overamped brain. Stroboscopic flashes! Tailored to your own brainscan dreamology. And, every time the song comes on the radio, the clip runs.

Movies—who needs them? Or MTV. Especially MTV. Too explicit to sustain the fantasy. Even in the abbreviated narrative of the script, the intertwining of fictional episodes always rings false. Movies have been a stumbling block to many a rock group, including the Stones and the Beatles. Elvis being the prime example. The *Bambi* movie dragged on. McLaren thought it should end with the Sex Pistols in-spiring an anarchist revolution that sweeps England.

Meanwhile, McLaren has been busy. In October of 1976, EMI signs the group, which issues one single, "Anar-chy in the U.K." Deleted in January. EMI gives them 40,000 pounds to terminate the contract. In March of '77 they sign with A&M who eventually give them 75,000 pounds to go away. McLaren is ecstatic: "I keep walking in and out of of-fices, being given checks. When I'm older and people ask me what I used to do for a living I shall have to say: 'I went in and out of doors getting paid for it.' "

In November 1977, *Never Mind the Bollocks* is released. The *Saturday Night Fever* soundtrack album is high in the charts, along with Fleetwood Mac's *Rumours* (number one for 31 weeks). There is an injunction against the *Bollocks* title on the grounds of obscenity. Yet another scandal for Malcolm to chalk up! But when the case is prosecuted, a lady judge finds in the Sex Pistols favor. *Bollocks*, she rules, is a fine old Saxon word.

AUGUST 24, 1977. Magistrates in Nottingham, two of 'em women, ruled today that the record sleeve of Never Mind the Bollocks is not indecent. They 'ad this ol' geezer, Professor Kinsley, testemonial that the word bollocks 'ad appeared in medieval bibles an 'as been 'eard uttered on more'n one occasion by no less than Prince Phillip 'isself. Further, it is in common parlance in Scandinavian an Germanic countries the meanin of which is a small bull.

Is this wot our disk title is likely to read in them countries, then, Never Mind the Small Bulls? Malcolm, 'oo was 'opin for a big kerfuffle over the matter, will be sorely disappointed. But I is well pleased wif the outcome. Thanks, dears. Drop round for a pint if you 'appen to be in the neighborhood of Pindock Muse, me new abode. Sophie Richmond 'as found me a flat in Maida Vale wif a seven-year lease which Malcolm sez is plenty long enough since I shall be dead by then. True enough. Show up at the office four hours late, wot you expect no fuckin alarm clock?

21
Vortex

Sɪᴅ ʜᴀᴅ ᴀ ᴄʟᴇᴀʀ, ʙᴏʟᴅ ᴏᴜᴛʟɪɴᴇ, ᴀ ᴄʜᴀʀᴀᴄᴛᴇʀ sᴛʀɪᴘᴘᴇᴅ ᴏғ the messy contradictions of real life. When you combine a short attention span with a broad outline what you have is caricature. Instantly identifiable Sid. Lydon dazzled. Sid horrified.

His performance consisted in presenting himself. Just that. The flaunting of a grotesque temperament on stage. He only had to *appear*. When you saw Sid, the Burroughsian Space Bug, you knew exactly what kind of sound went with this look.

By the time of the American tour in January 1978, Sid was a random destruction machine with no brakes. In the sweepstakes for the Most Maniacal Thing Alive, Sid won hands-down.

Sid is an aspect of Rotten that gets loose and goes on to take over the script—a now drastically simplified plot in which the stand-in ends up stealing the show. And why not? Sid is the world's leading Sexpistolologist. Maybe he knows more about them, can see the picture more clearly than they themselves. He's the quintessential rock fan who can repeat the dialogue word for word, the deranged visionary hell-bent on inserting himself into their mythology. And, let's face it, they do have serious third-act problems. Not to worry, Sid'll fix it. He even knows how it should all end.

This is Sid's gig. You can see right away the equilibrium of the group has shifted. It's no longer the lone raving nutter against a backdrop of Cook, Jones, and Matlock. With Sid in the group there's torque. Sid's pulling the center away from Rotten. Lydon is tugging it back. A coiled spring.

Sid assumes the position: legs splayed in spastic Gene Vincent gammy-leg stance, right arm poised in Townshend windmill pose—never mind that this scything gesture makes no sense for a bass player. Strike a pose! A compendium of mannerisms culled from fifties and sixties rock icons, comic books, fashion rags, horror movies, Eddie Cochran being the armature, the cybermanikin that holds all the flourishes together. Hey, you're something else, man!

Everything is distorted, slightly out of phase as if some proleptic vortex were morphing him into the future. Hair, wind-tunnel face contorted into Clint Eastwood snarl. Except that the Elvis-mutated-into-spaghetti-western sneer—on

Sid—doesn't quite stick. It's slipping, draining off the menace. The Kabuki actor in full makeup and regalia who hasn't quite got the eye-popping demon thing down yet. More Deputy Dawg than high-plains drifter. But this is all part of his thing—goofiness. Any teenager can do the menacing look. But menace plus goofy is tricky. It's never the straight macho with Sid. How could it be? Just a skinny, weedy kid.

Regardless of what posture they are currently fronting, Brit rock stars—Mick and Keith, Townshend, Bowie, even Lydon himself—are always at one remove. It's a sleight of hand. You don't—however spontaneous you appear to be— just willfully jump on the first runaway train, like Hendrix, Joplin, or Morrison. It's all fucking theater, dahling!

But within Punk there is a strain that's against the grain—distinctly un-Brit, un-removed. That mix of angsty existential ferocity of fifties rock, a Euro fetish for ideologies and the semantics of fashion plus wayward intensity. It's this very essence of out-of-controlness that Sid embodies: The urge to leap on the hood of the car going over the cliff.

Sid knew he was in trouble. For all intents and purposes an orphan (his mum a child herself), he was always looking for mothers and fathers. He first attached himself to Leee Black Childers. When he joined the Sex Pistols, Malcolm became the father figure. In that gothic family, Sid was McLaren and Westwood's favorite child. "Of all those who flocked to the pair's dream academy, Sid Vicious was the most vulnerable," says Jon Savage.

On the "Spots" tour he latches on to the driver, Barbara Harwood, asking her to "take him away and sort him out."

They play barely fifteen dates in the U.K. in 1977 (they don't have to), but eventually the Pistols are going to have to show what they've got, they are going to have to *prove it*. Things have got so hot in Britain that touring in the U.K. is out of the question. There are towns that won't even let them *in*. The only places left to tour are on the Continent. There are plenty of offers: Sweden, Norway, Finland, Holland, France . . . It's no longer just the U.K. that craves sacred monsters. We're talking a genuine international need. The whole tired old planet is bored. It wants to be insulted and spat upon, and lick the boots of the new beast.

> FREEZIN-COLD WINTER BLIZZARD WEATHER. WON'T EVEN LET US INTO THE BLOODY HOTEL, NEVER MIND PLAYIN THE GIG. END UP DOIN ABAWT SIX OUTTA EIGHTEEN GIGS.

And, now—the U.S.A., the great maw of novelty, has developed a sweet tooth for outrage, it wants to get in on the act. They, too, want a look-see at the Most Outrageous Thing Going. The American tour is to be the big crunch. This will be the defining moment for the Sex Pistols, for Punk itself.

But these guys can't even get out of the fuckin' U.K. without creating the proverbial "incident," havoc pursuing them even unto Heathrow Airport:

Wednesday, January 4, 1978

PUNK ROCK GROUP SHOCKS AIRPORT

The Sex Pistols flew out of Britain yesterday spitting and shouting abuse.

Police were called as passengers on their Pan-Am flight from Heathrow to New York complained about their behaviour.

Swinging punches and hiding their faces behind newspapers, the punk rock band turned their abuse mainly on photographers. "You are scum!" they shouted, and muttered threats about taking certain photographers down back alleys.

Very naughty lads indeed. Not simply street-pissers like the Rolling Stones but felons with yer actual rap sheets. All have police records: Sid, two counts of assaulting police officers, one stolen car; Lydon, possession of amphetamine sulfate; Cook and Jones, theft (multiple counts).

Andy Warhol knew a fine piece of spin-doctoring when he saw it: "The Sex Pistols arrived in the U.S.A. today. Punk

---

Envy is a terrible fing, innit? 'Ee knows full well that it makes not a fuckin iota of difference whevver I play me fuckin' bass or not. Me job is larkin abawt, innit? I play me own mesomeric spasm of claustrophobic angst, have me place where I can cavort, throw fings around. Wif five bloody camera crews an fifty photographers out there, it gets me juices flowin. But 'Is 'Ighness's nose is a bit outta joint an all. I reckon the old tosser's losin it. I fink you is jealous, Lydon my lad, that's wot I fink your problem is.

---

is going to be so big. They're so smart, whoever's running the tour, because they're starting where the kids have nothing to do, so they'll go really crazy."

22

Anarchy in the U.S.A.

Build your cities on the slopes of Vesuvius! Live in conflict with your equals and yourselves! Send your ships out into unchartered seas!

—FRIEDRICH NIETZSCHE

LESS THAN A YEAR IN THE BAND AND PUNK'S EXHIBIT A HAS JUST about taken over. El Sid is a fantasy-fueled engine whose deranged authority presides over the last kamikaze phase as the Sex Pistols crash and burn.

For American punks, Sid personifies the Sex Pistols. He's the runaway train they go down to the railway crossing to see careen through the barriers.

And out there, humming night and day, the tireless American media radar—a manic

> LOOK AWT, YA POXY YANKS, IT'S SID THE ID COMIN ATCHA!

insect with electronic feelers ceaselessly *scanning, scanning,*

scanning. Wide-screen U.S.A. can only identify very clear outlines. No problem about Sid showing up on it. He's a frenzied hieroglyphic signifying to the great public the wretched excess and wanton chaos of Punk. Punk as manic graphic. Furiously twitching mediated antennae glom on to Sid and suck

---

JANUARY 5. We open at a shoppin mall! Par for the fuckin course, eh mate? An the openin act's some stroppy psychedelic garage band called Merc-o-Matic. Wherever do they get these names from—the 7-Eleven? Every bleedin newspaper an TV station in the world's there for our great unveilin an we done wot we always does when under intense scrutiny—we stank! Steve's guitar outta tune, Rotten's voice 'opelessly flat. Fans don't even try to get onstage. Alas, no murder, mutilation, mayhem, or even one bloody gob. We is definitely loony bait, however! More fuckin narcs, hacks, an flacks on this poxy tour than there is audience, an lots of redneck cops just itchin to blow us away. This is the real people? Sod awf! Not to mention bloody rock writers swarmin all over the bus. Wankers! When Rotten asks the little buggers, "Aren't we the worse fing you ever seen?" the audience bloody cheers. They're eivver very hip, these cowboys, or fuckin idiots. An so to bed.

---

him in with their tractor beam.

Johnny Rotten is another story entirely. Too ironical, too complex, too *Brit*, basically, to get through. But Sid is perfect. A sharp, cartoonlike outline that caricatures Punk nihilism and wretched excess to a T. He's a deranged cartoon, devoid

of Rotten's shape-shifting ventriloquism. He's the Sex
Pistols' self-mashing mascot of transgres-sion. His reckless
self regard and devotion to the livefastdieyounghaveabeau-
tifulcorpse credo are cru-
cial to the mythology.

*Run animated se-
quences of:*

Ferocious Maya
glyph awoken out
of his millennial
cocoon—chattering
skull and jangling
skeleton—shaking a
death-rattle, spread-
ing the centipede
sickness.

**An . . . 'ello, wot's this, then?
A City of Atlanta squad car
screams up. Trigger-happy cops
leap out with guns at the ready.
Prepared to blow you away, son,
don't make no mistake about it.
For carryin liquor in a public
area? Hell, you limey suckers
don't know shit. True, very, very
true—thank god!**

Gibbering demon leaping from a medieval psalter
into a frenzy of quivering malevolence, now here
now there, leering, sneering, snarling, hurling,
bleeding, stomping, spitting, cursing and flashing
the two-fingered fuck you, and like a thing possessed ceaselessly tormenting the innocent and
simple, trampling on the graves of the righteous
and ridiculing their sanctimonious impotence.

Psychotic pixel that with fiendish haste rushes from
one side of the brain to the other like some hell-
spawned imp, shrieking, "Alarm! The sky is falling!

The mayor's gone mad, beauty parlor's going up in flames!"

Crank-crazed biker hun rampaging through shopping mall, raping, pillaging, pushing dope on kids and destroying appliances.

The Sex Pistols arrive in New York City on January 3, 1978, apocalyptic banners flying. What they play is irrelevant. News bites don't even bother with their music. Just shots of scrawny, mean-looking boys making menacing gestures to the camera. What it all means matters less than their immaculate front: a lethally tooled obnoxiousness. They are sexy, threatening, and drop-dead cool.

Their first show is at Atlanta's Great SouthEast Music Hall. Rotten in fine fettle: "You bleedin' bunch of statues. I've never seen an audience like you bleedin' rotters." Woah! It's the *audience* that is on trial. What carny arrogance! You poxy scum, let's see if you can live up *to our* expectations!

Rotten, in tails, comes up to the mike after "I Wanna Be Me" ("the new British National Anthem," says he) and has the brazen nerve to tell the audience to stop *looking* at him: "Stop staring and just start dancing. Have some fun. We're all ugly. We know that." Rotten Book of Quotes, number 134. When Sid slips out of his leather jacket to show his Belsen-like body with concave chest, Rotten points him out: "See the fine upstanding young men Britain's chucking out these days." Quote number 289. After twelve songs—ending with "Anarchy in the *U.S.A.*"—they pack it in. Mercifully, no encores.

Twelve days of Sodom and Gomorrah across the U.S.A. Tourism consists of souvenir shops, sex emporiums, the ghoulish and the kitsch. In Dallas, a visit to Boot Hill. In

So, disgusted wif this situation along wif me ongoin malaise abawt the disappearance of God, I inhales a pint of vodka an scarpers along the railroad tracks behind the club. Get a feel for America, know wot I mean? An a'course, sniff out our local needle park. Kidnapped by Ziggy Stardust friends, bomb around in a van wif sunset an waterfalls on it—lovely artwork. I ingest five hundred milligrams of, um, somefing. Pretty strong fuckin shit! Aaaaaah, this is more like it, as Dr. Jekyll said. Feelin no pain, I requests a carvin knife. Wot for? For body enhancement, ya stupid cunt, wot you fink? Really, these Yanks is so dense. I'll indulge in a little self-mutilation if nobody minds. Cut a nice big rasher outta me chest. Next mornin, recaptured alas! Now the fuckin roadies won't let me out of their sight. Malcolm's spoutin awf abawt people that is followin us around. Wot the fuck do you fink, Malcolm? A'course, they're followin us around, that's the 'ole point of the fing, innit? The band 'ave sent me to Coventry. Sod awf! If me minder finks 'ee's gonna shake me willy an put it away afterwards 'ee's got anuvver fink comin.

> **DEAR DIARY:** Must mention gettin a blow job in the loo from a black sex-change in a blonde bouffant. Also, in-store appearances is always mad fun. Rotten an meself running through the record shop, grabbin everyfing we can lay our hands on, sign a few autoscribbles, come out wif hundreds of fuckin dollars' worth of merchandise which we soon grow bored of an throw out the window of the bus halfway down the road. Childish but necessary activity if our spirits is to remain buoyant!

Austin, the University of Texas Clock Tower (where Charles Whitman shot forty-five people with a high-powered rifle). In Memphis, the obligatory trip to Graceland.

From the window of the bus, American surrealism in ac-

> **JANUARY 6.** Plane struck by lightnin on flight to Memphis. An apocalyptic portent, clearly. Fuckin 'ell! Iz that a omen or wot? Religious wankers would love that: GODLESS PUNK ROCKERS STRUCK DOWN BY HAND OF ALMIGHTY! I wakes up next mornin, bored an anxious, nuffin to fuckin do, is there, an I seen all the cartoon shows already. Findin little else purposeful, I slope off to suss out the dope scene down Beale Street. Would you believe it? Fuckin gun-totin 'ippies find me stoned poolside an beat the shit outta me. Muvver's milk to me, actually. I like gettin beatin up, 'ow else am I supposed to make friends? It's 'ow I bond, ya gormless prat! Wot irks is the fuckin hygiene business. Fillin a bathtub an puttin me in it. If someone treats you like a baby you regress! Waaaah.

tion. Neon cactuses, snake farms, lassoing motel signs, Injun knickknack trading posts, truck stops and donut shops, jackknifed semis spilling out their cargo of watermelon blood and guts, cowboys in ten-gallon hats, and Dolly Parton look-alikes with polyester hair.

The hypostatized geography of Texas, Louisiana, Georgia, Oklahoma. A demon-infested panorama with alternating tableaux of dislocation. Phantasmagoria of American roadside nightlife with that quirky twist the South puts on it. That 35-degrees out-of-kilter Dixie torque that makes everything that little bit more freaky.

> **JANUARY 8, SAN ANTONIO. DEAR DIARY:**
>
> **I WAKES UP TO THE VILE STRAINS OF "BURNIN' LOVE" ON THE TELLY. IT'S THE KING'S ANNIVERSARY. HALF A YEAR UNDERGROUND, OLD DARLIN. MANY 'APPY RETURNS, EL!**

Rotten and Vicious sauntering through a car park next to the motel, on their way to Tattletales to catch a little tits 'n' arse. Dingy transvestite clubs in shopping malls. Hard-nut shitkickers dressed up like Southern belles or Little Bo Peep in a miniskirt. Little cubicles in the back where they show hard-core triple-X–rated porno loops and little trannies in Belle Rive gowns down on their knees giving it away.

Diversions on the road. Spackling the Warner Bros. artist-development guy's tie and jacket with ketchup and mustard, throwing snot-drenched tissues at him and pretending to throw up on him.

Sid cut off from his usual supply. Cold turkey, no way to score, panic setting in. To avoid temptation, they skip New

York. Sid spends most of the tour crashing, getting sick, drinking peppermint schnapps. Stuck to the toilet seat, hours-old vomit in his mouth. He's virtually under motel arrest, repeatedly beaten up by gun-toting hippie security, who also wash him like a baby. Paranoia escalates with the arrival of Tom Forcade (publisher of *High Times*) and entourage, including a film crew with Lech Kowalski directing his documentary of doom, *D.O.A.*

> **MALCOLM'S TELLIN US THAT TOM FORCADE IS A BLOODY CIA/DEA/FBI AGENT, BUT TOM DON'T 'AVE THE REGULATION WHITE GOLF SHOES, DO 'EE, SO I DAWT IT. VERY STRICT ABAWT THE FASHION CODE THE FBI IS. IMPERSONATIN A FEDERAL AGENT, WHAT A WALLY!**

Sid has taken to carving desperate messages on his chest. Nothing too fancy: GIMME A FIX.

> **MONDAY, JANUARY 9. The Family Inn, Baton Rouge. Dear Diary:**
> **Fan gives me I'M A MESS button. Very appropriate, too, if I might say so. 'Umiliation bein a matter of pride wif me, heh, heh. Annuvver bloody stoopid concert wif everybody frowin pig's snouts an trotters onstage tonite—fuckin Li'l Abner shit. Back at the motel, Noel fuckin Monk-the-Cunt 'as tore out the bloody phone! "Wot's this, then?" I asks, all hurt. Fer me own good, 'ee says. Sod awf!**

Given the cast of characters, there are bound to be little cultural misunderstandings with the locals.

Rotten:

Sid loved to approach these Dolly Parton look-alikes and their trucker boyfriends with their big cowboy hats. There would be fights at the redneck truck stops. They would stand up and say, "I think you insulted my wife!"

Sid, of course, didn't have the common sense to back down and say, "No, I didn't, and sorry if you think so." He'd say something daft like, "I think your wig is an insult enough." To Sid it was all just fashion statements. He didn't realize these people lived and died by their hairdos. Just like Sid himself. He didn't have that kind of street education where you move on so you don't get your head whacked.

This 'ere Tom Forcade 'ooever 'ee is—some fuckin Yip-pie/hippie herbert wif a entourage of lads, liggers, an rock 'n' roll poseurs—reminds me of the arties an social-realist mob that used to follow us around. The tosser's of-ferin me 'is Chinese muscle men as protection against the Warner security goons. Wants to furnish me wif a lifetime supply of bicycle chains so as I might strike back. The naff 'ippie misunderstands the situation utterly.

An animated S. Clay Wilson comic-book sequence:

Gnarled old cowboy sitting at nearby booth. Fat beer-belly, chicken-fried-steak gravy dribbling down chin, barbed-wire whiskers, mean whiskey eyes. "Vicious, that your name, son?" Extinguishing cigarette on rawhide hand. "Jus' exaggly how Vicious are ya?" Sneering shitkicker you-li'l-limey-faggot leer spreading across face. Taunting you, Sid, challenging you, seeing if you've got any *cajones*. 'Strooth! The metacreature is endangered, his very essence threatened by some trucker from Abilene.

Sid has seen too many John Wayne flicks; the cowboy has read too many lurid tabloid accounts of Punks. Battle of the mediated demons! Sid's relentless mythomania won't permit him to see in front of him a tired old trucker on his night out who's had a few too many Wild Turkeys. He sees Black Bart, *High Noon*, Jack Palance in *Shane*. It's a showdown at the truck-stop café. He's gotta show this galoot who's the toughest dude in Texas or hightail it outta the territory. A quasidemonic power comes over him. He is invincible—like, you know, Megaman X. Isn't Sid Vicious a larger-than-life action figure, a superhero as outlandish, as outsized, as any Paul Bunyan or Mike Fink? Sid takes out his knife and *very slowly* slices open a huge gash on his hand, letting the blood drip down on his steak and eggs. The cowboy takes his wife and kid and leaves the joint pronto. El Sid has measured himself against the mythical Southern cowboy and he has not been found wanting.

El Sid

Or a chapter "In Which Sid Makes Some New Buddies":

Sid's punching one of the roadies. Sneaky little jabs to the body. *Whack! Whack! Pow!* But don't hurt none. EX lets Sid go at him for a few minutes. Shit, he's drunk, he's scrawny. Ain't gonna do *too* much damage. But, fuck, if the little fucker won't quit...! This is getting mighty *irritatin'*. Okay, cut the shit! He pulls Sid off him, grabs him by his hair and bangs his head hard against the sink a half-dozen times. Sid slumps to the floor, holding his head. "Okay, okay," he says, "now we can be friends."

23

The San Antonio Triptych

S ID ONSTAGE AT R ANDY'S R ODEO. H E'S LIT-UP LIKE A THOUSAND Christmas-tree lights. Holding his bass as if it were a miniature cross. Li'l Sid, his metal-and-wood doppelgänger who never needs to eat or sleep and whose cry is a basso rumble, a metallic throb.

The more Rotten/Lydon withdraws—to short-circuit audiences' expectations—the more Sid hogs the spotlight and the larger the Sid metacreature grows. (You recall Bertolt Brecht's *Verframdungeffekt*, don'tcha? Well, this is the Finsbury version of that.)

Like mild-mannered Dr. Bruce Banner, he's been

changed utterly into his own mutated Hulk. Buried alive inside Sid the Id. Any saving inconsistencies between himself and his new incarnation get ditched when he dumps his former selves, Simon Ritchie and John Beverley, down an elevator shaft. Without them Sid is a hydroponic personality, a fantasy creature as ungrounded and voracious as a ghost.

Did I tell ya that I got me own minder? Yeah, I do. Nah, not Boogie. Boogie's a lost soul, like me! It's that ferret, Noel Monk.

First appearance of the wanker not exactly promisin. First fing inna mornin I got to listen to 'im whinin, "Listen, maaan, would you please take a fucking shower?" What is this cleanliness mania anyways? It's so bloody Yank, all this Mr. Clean shit. 'Ee's goin on like a bleedin TV advert. An 'im smokin 'is filthy sixpenny cigars like a chimney stack. An wot a way to treat the talent, I arsk you. The worst of it 'avin to listen to Mr. Big Cigar dronin on abawt 'is "priorities." To wit: "Hey, maaan, if you wanna have a drink or smoke a joint or something, fine, but THERE WILL BE NO HARD DRUGS ON MY TOUR. That clear?" His tour? A misunderstandin, surely! Everybody in the band hatin each uvver already, an we've only bin 'ere two days. Malcolm not doin a bloody fing, hidin out under the covers in 'is room. Love the silly bugger. Got the courage of 'is convictions, that one.

The Sid metacreature has its own logic, a larger-than-life entity whose acts need to be proportionately extreme and superhuman—a hypotrophic cartoon—something out of Marvel Comics. And Sid is a big Marvel fan. He communes daily with these cosmic entities, his peers, immersing himself in their intergalactic battles. Creations of a fevered brain! Galacticus! Dr. Strange! The Silver Surfer! Thor! Now here are worthy models—the unstoppable ones—like El Sid. And the pervy little solipsist seems to identify utterly with his creature—the

> VERY NICE ERUPTION. WHEN A YOUNG TEXAN . . . IDIOT TRIES TO EXPRESS 'IS DISAGREEMENT, I CLUBS 'IM WIF ME BASS GUITAR AND ALL 'ELL BREAKS LOOSE.

all-powerful, all-conquering . . . Vicious Man!

This—the magic capacity, the irradiating superpower—has always been his fervent wish. To transcend his pathetic self and become a character of dauntless human power! An entity so monstrous it *revels* in self-laceration. A sort of heavy-metal martyr, mutilation being a kind of religious mania that rejects the body, denies its existence, a kind automartyrdom.

Rotten's taken to calling him "Sid fuckin' Useless," but however much his mates in the band shake their heads and say "wot a bleedin' shame it is wot's 'appened to Sidney," they still need him, no doubt about it. The nihilism and frenzy of the Sex Pistols is embedded in the Sid character. For the fans he is the Sex Pistol incarnate.

I really don't know why they're all picking on Sid because it seems to me that he was the only one

keeping up the usual Sex Pistol spirit in America.
I thought he looked beautiful with his face and
chest covered in blood.

letter from Shirley X

As the Pistols thrash across America spinning vile and repulsive tales, their dark legend breeds fantastic stories. Even
the cynical PR guys from Warner Bros. are impressed. When
Rotten says he'll tear their heads off and eat their brains their
reaction is: "Wow, we've got genuine monsters here!"

And don't forget Malcolm McLaren, skulking in his
hotel room as his little savages cavort before the cameras.
He's the premier exporter of Anglo-Saxon oddities this year,
but like any other Brit confronted with the vast unruly continent that produced baggies and bug bras, he's conflicted.
The utter disdain for most things American is tempered by
an almost quasi-religious reverence for the legendary Southern landscape, the source of all real things. Blues, jazz, rock
'n' roll, movies, hominy grits, pecan pie, Holiday Inns (one
of whose early investors was the same man who first
recorded Elvis and Jerry Lee—none other than Sam Phillips
himself).

McLaren had at first thought of opening the tour at the
Apollo Theater in Harlem and then moving on to Mississippi
(with twice-blessed Tupelo being one of the possible stops).
Even the revised itinerary is dripping with Southern mythology: Memphis, San Antonio, Baton Rouge, Dallas, Tulsa. Sacred sites! The English salivate over the mere mention of
such names. But these aren't by any stretch of the imagina-

tion rock 'n' roll venues. Mainly country-music corrals, like the one tonight at Randy's Rodeo, a converted bowling alley filled with two thousand rowdy Texans who pelt the band as soon as they come onstage.

Hot dogs, popcorn, beer cans coming at them from all sides. Indians fighting Mexicans, Mexicans fighting cowboys. The Alamo and Custer's Last Stand and all of them thinking, What the fuck is this limey shit? The only reason WWIII

MALCOLM IN 'IS INFINITE WISDOM 'AS DECIDED WE'RE TO PLAY FOR "REAL PEOPLE," WHATEVER THAT MAY BE. COWBOYS, MEXICANS, REDNECKS, SOUTHERN SHERIFFS. LOVELY! ONE FING'S FOR SURE, WIF REAL PEOPLE LIKE THESE, MAXIMUM AGGRO IS ALMOST AS GOOD AS GUARANTEED. AM LOOKIN FORWARD TO SOME LOVELY VIOLENT EPISODES.

doesn't break out is that the large Mexican contingent decide they *like* these fuckin' loco gringos.

Midway into the set, Sid bonks the sheriff with a bottle of Jack Daniel's and damned if the little fucker doesn't go for his gun. Sid gets a full beer can in the kisser. A redneck takes umbrage at being called a faggot and Sid clobbers him with his bass.

SHOWDOWN AT RANDY'S RODEO
*Sid turns Vicious as the Sex Pistols
battle with U.S. fans*

Sheriff's deputies rushed the stage as beer tins and bottles were hurled from the audience and the Pistols lashed back with curses, spit—and their instruments during the ugliest scenes of their U.S. tour.

The "shoot-out" at Randy's Rodeo, notorious for its tough customers, began after guitarist Sid Vicious provoked the audience by saying: "You cowboys are all faggots."

His gibe was met with an artillery of beer cans, many of them still full.

CRUMBS

Vicious was hit several times in the face with the tins. "That beer can hit me right in the mouth. It hurt but I don't care. Come on, what ya waitin for?" he said, inciting the crowd.

Living up to his name he lashed back after being hit with a pie thrown from the front row.

With crumbs still sticking to his face he swung wildly wielding his bass guitar like an ax and striking the pie thrower twice in the head as the man turned to leap onto the stage. He was seized and led away in handcuffs.

"Oh, dear, Sidney has dropped his guitar," said lead singer, Johnny Rotten.

Outside, the pie thrower, 32-year-old Name Withheld, shouted as police led him away: "I don't like what they stand for. They are just sewer rats with guitars."

Just the sort of flash McLaren's been waiting for. He's been sorely disappointed so far. Here he has America's Most Wanted Disaster rolling down the tracks, he's throwing them to the wind, and it isn't causing the storm he wanted. The papers still running that jerky PUNK ROCK COMES TO TOWN article.

Headline in morning's paper: PISTOLS WIN THE SAN AN-TONIO SHOOT-OUT.

Even the roadies are appalled at the band's behavior, yet oddly enough the band don't (as yet) indulge in the traditional rock-band ritual of trashing motel rooms. A reaction to the wankers of the sixties, no doubt. Biggest bill so far is $68.65 for motel damages: one shredded bedspread, one destroyed lampshade, and labor on glass cleaning. Nothing compared to the Who and Led Zeppelin.

Sid's out to change all that. Acquires a pair of brass knuckles which he tries out by punching holes in motel-room walls. Less than a week in the States and the Pistols have been banned from American Airlines and the Holiday Inn chain. Well, about fucking time.

Pistols hysteria on the nightly news. Walter Cronkite intones the words "Sid Vicious" in the same voice he might use for "the siege of Stalingrad." Well, if the daddy of all newscasters thinks this is "of grave concern," it can't be all bad. It's wild, it's new, it's guaranteed to exasperate your parents. It's the invasion of the body snatchers. Kids transforming themselves with safety pins, spiked hair cuts, and ugliness. Musk cologne. Pierced nipples. Leather bras. Dried-blood lipstick. The Sex Pistols are now a freak show, a diorama devised by Francis Bacon where distortion is the norm. And the least stable, the most gullible member of the band is slowly getting more and more twisted out of shape.

A carload of punks have made the journey from L.A. to

Dallas to see the agony of their holy martyr. When rock is really cooking, there's always one madman out there dancing on the third rail. This year it's Sid. He's got it, the *oubajowa* power, the X factor. Isn't that what rock 'n' roll is all about? The derailed thing careening down the two-lane blacktop at 120 mph, screaming out of the window at the top of its lungs. Little Richard, Jerry Lee Lewis, Elvis, Eddie Cochran—all charter members of the Hysterical Order of Manic Hegelians for Holy Automartyrdom. Fuck common sense. We have come for the games.

The Longhorn Ballroom, Dallas, January 10, 1978. Sid punching his bass guitar strings with his wrists. Midway through the second song, three broken strings (a bass only has four to begin with). Playing on *one* string—what a genius! The guitar is just a prop, anyway. Like Saint Catherine with her fiery wheel, or Elvis in Las Vegas, acoustic slung around his neck like an oversized medallion.

Helen Killer shares vodka with Sid, French-kisses him, each time more passionately, during "New York." She gets up onstage, leans her body closer to Sid, falling on her knees in front of him. A gesture of reverence, abasement, devotion. But this is a pagan ritual, Babylonian, even. A temple prostitute, the sacred whore of Ra! Sid twists his bass behind him giving her access to his crotch. She has his jeans halfway down to the floorboard before the promoter calls Monk to pull her off—to the dismay of Sid and Helen and all those who came to watch.

To the dismay of Lydon, too, because he sees his pan-

tomime of rage turned into a sideshow: "Uh, Sidney? Whenever you're ready, Sidney."

**Well, well, an wot do I spy wif my little eye but some sub-
teen bondage crumpet climbin the stairs in me direction.
An, anon, after exchangin banalities they enters me parlor. "Ladies," I sez. "We ain't ladies," they sez, all butch
like, an so I goes, "Waa'l, obviously you ain't. It's a fuckin
joke now, innit?" Not too much upstairs, I'm afraid. "Wot
you fuckin' sluts want, then, a bit of the old in-out?"
"We're not like that," they sez. "So wot youse doin in me
room an all, then?" "We want your autograph," they sez,
all innocent an dewy. I love this fuckin stoopid game! I
pull out the fuckin giant, monstrous Bowie knife I bought
in Atlanta, an sez wif a wicked grin, "Where you want it,
then?" "You as bad as they say?" they ask. "Watch this,
you fuckin sorry bitches," I sez, an cuts a great slash on
me arm which drips evilly onto the orange shag carpet.
"Oooo!" they go, "can we lick it?" I send the fat one with
the racoon eyes out to get pizza an 'ave positioned meself on top of the skinny one fully dressed (I am getting a
bit kinky this way) an she is given me head when—ooops!
From feebleness due to goin' cold-turkey I puke all over
the cunt an 'ave to enlist that wally Noel's help in goin out
to buy her some new clothes. 'Ee really loves that as you
might imagine. Sulks out the door, an just to aggravate
'im a bit more, I goes, "Size nine, darlin, an somefing
saucy, if you don't mind."**

Midway through "Problems," a teenage suicide-blonde
punk, leather wristband ringed with barbed wire in the front

row is screaming, "SID! SID! FUCKIN' SID VICIOUS! FUCK YOU!" Sid, ever the curious one, leans over, until he gets close enough to her face. Closer, closer until his cheek is right next to hers. And suddenly, like a blonde cobra, she rears her head back and slams it into his, opening a gash on his nose. Blood mingles with saliva. Helen Killer headbutts him repeatedly on the nose. But he gives as good as he gets, does Sid. *Whack!* Kicks her in the head. Blood spurts out. She sees it gushing from her head. She's been blessed.

He lets it flow all over his chest like war paint. Blood on his chest, blood streaming out of his nose. He rips a pus-soaked bandage off his arm, revealing a pus-oozing gash and throws the putrid piece of gauze to the crowd who fight over it like bridesmaids over a bouquet. The blood is now running into his mouth. He spits it on the front row. Little red flecks splatter the faces of the punkettes, eager for benediction. They are in ecstasy. But it's a never-ending job, this blood-letting business. While spitting blood at the front row his bloody nose has begun to coagulate. The blood is starting to dry up! Something must be done right away. Sid goes over to his amp, shatters a bottle of whiskey and begins cutting his chest.

Self-laceration nightly! You will actually see the blood of the Holy Martyr Vicious dripping from his chest! Splash it on you, smear it on your face as a talisman against the evil eye. Take home a vial as a souvenir from our reliquary shop. No pig's blood or Revlon movie goop substitutes employed. Only authentic Vicious Plasma™ used.

Helen Killer and the ghoulish coven of punkettes

haven't come to see just another rock 'n' roll show, they're here for this—the blood sport. The most outrageous rock 'n' roll sideshow in the world—Sid the geek, LIVE! ON-STAGE! Forget about KISS and Ozzy Osbourne or even Alice. This is the real thing—Sid covered in blood mixed with Heineken, pus, and mustard, and the stage knee-deep in bottles, cans, and garbage. Apotheosis! Epiphany! Canon-ization! You may now enter the Hall of Pop Martyrs—James Dean, Elvis, Marilyn, Hendrix, Joplin, Morrison. The price? Hey, we can discuss price later.

Dallas Morning News: "Most of the people last night came to see the people who came to see the Sex Pistols". Uh-huh.

January 12, Tulsa and points west. Dilatory bus chat:

> ROTTEN: Sid-nay, I wish you would apply yourself to writin songs again. We 'ave a total of eleven songs in our entire oeu-vre. It's embarrassin.
>
> SID: Wot you mean? New material pourin outta me all the time, mate. I just written a song about South Africa about how the niggers is gonna rise up, and annuvver one abawt God. It's a real attack, it's a death march.
>
> ROTTEN: It's gettin bawrin, Sid-nay, go on about the royals, Sid, or somefin.
>
> SID: Nah, there's no percentage in it. She's just an ol' boiler in a tiarer, ain't she? But look 'ere, John, in *Cream* we is bein' touted as the new Rolling Stones.
>
> ROTTEN: How vile!

SID: Know wot I fink? Keef Richard's nuffin' but a pathetic ol' vampire junkie that goes to get 'is fuckin' blood changed. He ought to change his bloody face, I'd do it for 'im at no extra charge.

ROTTEN: Oh, pathetic junkie, is it?

SID: Don't say junkie.

ROTTEN: Junkie, junkie, junkie, junkie!

Sid passes out while drinking peppermint schnapps. Coming into Los Angeles a roadie wakes him.

Good morning, Noel, may I see your lovely knife? Wot a big knife you 'ave, Noel. I 'ave 'arf a inclination to cut a 'arf-inch gash on me arm an, followin' the advice of the Divine Oscar, I gives in to the temptation. Lovely—instant cunt. Naturally I am anxious to show off me new body art to me mate John but the blagger susses right away: "Oh look," hisseth Rotten, " 'ere comes Mr. Drug. 'Allo, Mr. Drug, finkin about perhaps showin up for the performance tonight, Sid-nay?" Wot are friends for, I arsk you? Always windin me on is John, but I must remain above the fray. Ignorin the intended rudeness I sashay toward the bus between Jones an Cook. " 'Allo sidemen, 'ow does it feel to be part of the backin band?" To which they responds wif their squirmy li'l monkey chant: "Junkie! Junkie! Junkie!" But it don't bovver me none.

24

If You're Going to San Francisco . . .

Onward rolls the circus of the damned toward the hippie stronghold, San Francisco. Here the final conflict is to take place—Pop Armageddon!—the battle for reality between hippies and Punks will be decided at the Winterland Ballroom. McLaren the ideologist has chosen the venue vengefully, the idea being: Let's do a San Francisco show and shove it to the hippies (who, like, by this time have all moved out to Marin County).

Sid and Rotten make a quick trip to a gay sex shop for leather-studded nasties and lubricant. Sid lathers his hair with K-Y jelly for that spiky look. "Great, Sid," says Rotten. "Now you can stick your head up somebody's arse."

Then on to KSAN. The *Bonnie Simmons Show.* The usual abuse and obtuseness from Lydon. He and Sid only show up at the interview because they've been promised leather jackets for good behavior.

SIMMONS: Some people call Iggy Pop the godfather of Punk.

ROTTEN: I call 'im an ol' toss-pot.

SIMMONS: Well, who do you like?

ROTTEN: Me.

SIMMONS: I would hope so, anybody else?

Rotten: Nah, not really, not at all. I don't like rock music. I don't even know why I'm in it. It's just the only way I can destroy things. It's the best way. Have I earned my leather jacket yet?

I sees it emblazoned in me mind like huge headlines in the *Sun*: DEATH THREATS DOG SEX PISTOLS. But wait a fuckin minute, on second perusal, there's somefin dodgy wif this. These death threats are too cinematic, if y'know wot I mean. The writer of these here purported notes is, in my 'umble estimation, not a God-obsessed, snake-molestin redneck driven berserk by rumors of rampant hedonism among our youth. A hedonism perpetrated by smut-pedalin, sushi-eatin record executives. Nah. This death-threat nonsense is clearly the doin's of none other than the Artful Dodger 'isself. This is a nice development—one's own bloody manager manufacturin death threats! Wishful finkin on Malcolm's part, obviously.

Rotten doing his characteristic bilious rant. Brilliant! In the U.K., it's expected. It's the only thing they understand—

Luddites, ranters, the nutter on his apple box at Hyde Park Corner raving on. It's entertaining for the Yanks, too. But what's all this slagging each other off? Rotten trashing Sid, Sid trashing McLaren, McLaren slandering his own band, everybody in the group hating each other's guts and yelling it out at anybody who'll listen. Even on the bloody stage.

FUCK AWF IS THE WORD I WAS LOOKIN' FOR. THANK YOU, DAVE (ME INVISIBLE WORD COUNSELOR). WOT THEY PUT IN THIS FUCKIN DRINK, THEN, ANYWAY? WINDEX? BLUE VODKA, THAT'S A NEW ONE. OH, YEAH, THE DEATH THREATS.

Also, trashing interviewers is "not the business way." Americans are not going to understand this stuff at all. It doesn't play on the *Good Guy's Show* or in Wayne's World, for that matter. It's downright un-American. You're meant to chat up reporters, hand out PR releases, grease the deejays with an eight-ball of coke, set up junkets, lay on groaning buffets.

Sid slopes off to find dope. Arrives at the show way fucked-up. Bill Graham's Winterland is the biggest place the Sex Pistols have ever played (5,000 seats). Perfect for the final nosedive.

Despite being high on smack, Sid gets the show off to a decent start. He opens with two Ramones riffs, "Down in the Basement" and "Blitzkrieg Bop." Fans in the front row toss the appropriate offerings (syringes) on the stage. It's all downhill from there.

"I think it's fun. Do you want your ears blown out more?" Rotten asks peevishly. The sound is so distorted only

Rotten's vocal and Cook's drums cut through. Jon Savage, describing a tape of the concert, says, "Vicious is not so much out of tune and rhythm as on a different planet: the reports of his flailed bass punctuate the songs like far-off explosions."

> **AN NOW, TA-DAH! WOT DO WE 'AVE HERE BUT DEATH THREATS! OOOOO, WE ARE RIGHT SCARED O' THAT, I CAN TELL YOU. ALMOST PEED ME PANTS, I DID.**

It's a zombie performance but no matter, the fans don't care. Willy-nilly the Sex Pistols are caught up in a rock 'n' roll Möbius loop. Like others before them, they've become everything they set out to attack—cordoned off by bouncers, carted about in limos, surrounded by body guards, a stage ten feet above the heads of the audience. They've turned into mere purveyors of the despised situationist *spectacle*. Roll up! Roll up! Catch yer poxy Punks performin' perverse and vile acts—tonight, one show only!

But, hey, what kind of a performance would you want for a Sex Pistols finale? A note-perfect rendition of *Never Mind the Bollocks*? That would be a travesty, wouldn't it? Even a "good" performance would be a bit of a letdown wouldn't it? It's catch-22 because when they fuck up they do it gloriously and when they put on a good show they're just another act. To McLaren, anyway, they've become Led Zeppelin. What worse taunt could he think of?

Hadn't this been their goal all along? To crack the carapace of all that fussy rock formality—stagecraft, talent, pandering to the audience? *We can't play, we can't sing, we're not here for your entertainment, anyhow, so sod awf!*

In the end they do what comes naturally, they fuck up. Rotten, as usual, manages to turn the tables by critiquing the audience: "Tell us what it's like to have bad taste." His parting shot as he leaves the stage (and ends his book) is: "Ever get the feeling you've been cheated?"

Backstage is haunted. Cue the spectral voice of Lord Jim intoning "The End." A

BEFORE THE WINTERLAND, GET MESELF A WHOLE PARCEL OF HEROIN AN RIGHT BUGGER MESELF UP. GOOD FUCKIN RIDDANCE TO BAD RUBBISH. IT'S A BLOOMIN SHAMBLES ANYHOW, WHY SHOULD I TAKE THE FARCE SERIOUSLY WHEN NO ELSE'S PREPARED TO?

doomed quality hangs in the air. "You felt like asking them if they wanted to split for a beer," says party animal Legs McNeil, "but the Sex Pistols never dropped the pose."

> The Pistols sucked at Winterland but it didn't seem to matter. Everybody was just so thrilled to be in the presence of the Sex Pistols. . . . Every one of them looked miserable. Sid sat in a chair with his shirt off. Johnny was alone on a couch muttering to himself. Steve and Paul were lounging next to a garbage pail filled with Heinekens. Sid had pulled four chicks from the audience, and the four girls were just standing around. Everyone was ignoring them. Sid turned to one of them and said, "So, who's gonna fuck me tonight?"

Freeze-frame, but no pictures, please. Annie Liebowitz arriving like Van Dyke to paint their portrait is given short shrift.

After the show Sid disappears with the punkettes who've followed him from Dallas, and ODs in a shooting gallery in the Haight-Ashbury (a bit of irony here somewhere). Cook and Jones find him almost lifeless, turning blue on a mattress, a needle dangling from his arm. They walk him around. Take him to an acupuncturist. Sid proceeds to demolish the good doctor's house.

At five a.m. Sid, incoherent, calls Lydon to tell him he's disgusted with the group and especially with him.

> **POST-GIG BANTER:**
> **SID: WOT A FUCKIN BLOWOUT, MAN!**
> **ROTTEN: 'OW WOULD YOU KNOW?**
> **YOU IS SO BLOODY STONED ALL THE TIME, YOU WOULDN'T KNOW IF WE WAS PLAYIN "FREE BLIND MICE." AND IF I AM NOT MISTAKEN THAT WAS "FREE BLIND MICE" YOU WAS PLAYIN, WEREN'T IT?**

The two Hamlets (now not speaking to each other) show up one after the other in McLaren's room. McLaren claims to have lost interest in the group.

First Sid arrives. He needs money to buy some Mandrax (Quaaludes). When McLaren doesn't cough up, Sid turns into Rumpelstiltskin, flies into a rage, jumping on top of the dresser, kicking out the mirror, glass flying in his face, cursing his Svengali ("You're going to die for what you've done") and stalks out.

Then Lydon shows up, ranting. "You been stitching me up ever since you met me, stitch me up wif people beatin' me up, telling lies about me and now you want to put me on a plane with Sid. You're not talkin' to some idiot who coshed somebody on the train." McLaren accuses Lydon of turning into Rod Stewart. A low blow, that. But Lydon, never at a loss for invective, is right back at him. He charges McLaren with trying to turn him into Rod Stewart.

On the morning of the sixteenth, McLaren, Cook, and Jones fly to Brazil to film a segment of the *Sex Pistols'* ongoing film project with British train robber Ronnie Briggs (hence Lydon's gibe about the cosher). Rotten takes off for New York.

Glitterbest issues a statement: "The management is bored with managing a successful rock 'n' roll band. The group is bored with being a successful rock 'n' roll band. Burning venues and destroying record companies is more creative than making it."

The band that claimed its goal was to destroy rock 'n' roll had itself self-destructed.

And that, as they say, was that—the official end of the Sex Pistols and, for all intents and purposes, of Punk rock. But just as well, the Sex Pistols are at the end of their charge anyway. They'd been a parody of their former selves for over a year now. Quitting was the only decent thing to do, "even if," as Roberta Bailey put it, "they didn't do it for all the reasons we could have wished they did it."

Never mind. Their kamikaze plunge only adds to the legend. Not for them the long, drawn-out "career" along with the humiliating comebacks. Well, awright, *one* comeback tour after eighteen years is acceptable. But even then you run the risk of petty humiliations like the *New York Post* describing the Sex Pistols 1996 as: "Green Day on Geritol."

> **MALCOLM 'AS ANUVVER BRIGHT IDEA. 'EE'S GONNA RING UP CHARLIE MANSON. BRILLIANT, THEN WE'D 'AVE GENUINE BONIFIED MAYHEM ON THE TOUR AN THAT AIN'T ALL! WANTS MR. CHARLIE TO TAKE PART IN THE FILM, PERHAPS—OR WORSE—'EE RECKONS TO GET 'IM TO PRODUCE OUR NEXT RECORD. FROM PRISON NO LESS. WARDEN, BE A GOOD CHAP AN DIAL THE STUDIO FOR ME, I'VE GOT TO DO SOME OVERDUBBING ON THAT LAST MIX.**

What could be more compromising than the pathetic attempts of most groups who outlive their welcome to keep the thing going at any cost, tottering through another tour, another album (Procul Harum made seventeen). The strain of keeping up with the latest thing. "We've got to have a disco/reggae/rap number on our new album."

Have some decency, sirs, go out with a bit of pride intact. Find yourself an Abyssinia! Because, O my brothers, what could be worse than to degrade, to compromise, that original flash of the spirit? An abomination to man and god. Don't forget that in the end all will be called into question. Do you want to end up like the Grateful Dead?

Not the Sex Pistols. They go down in glorious flames. The very model of a Punk band as a paradigm of rock flash-urge-spurt. Flash point and vanish should be the prototype for all rock groups.

Run vidclip of Rotten at CBGB's. Sitting at the bar drinking a Heineken wearing a T-shirt that reads, I SURVIVED THE SEX PISTOLS TOUR—underneath he's handwritten, "*But the Band Didn't.*"

While Lydon announces the end of the group, Sid ODs on 80 mg of methadone and six or seven Valiums on the red-eye to New York. He slips into a drug-induced coma.

In a phone conversation with Roberta Bailey, from Jamaica Hospital, he explains his present condition (pharmacologically):

> SID: What happened was I done eighty milligrams of methadone, right, and when you get about six or seven Valiums, and you get high in the air, it has a much greater effect on you than when you're on the ground. You get pissed a lot quicker when you're in the air.

and otherwise:

> I don't fink anyone wanted to continue but nobody actually had the guts to actually say it so I just phoned John up and told him wot I thought of him, and where I thought he was at, and, erm, I mean I still fink I'm pretty good. I fink I was better than any of the others.

Bailey tries to tell him he could change, but he knows himself too well.

> SID: If I went out anywhere I wouldn't be able to resist the temptation, that would be the trouble. I'll end up burning myself out. Even in London the same thing. I'll probably die in six months actually. I can't straighten out, I can't be straight.

BAILEY: Yeah you could, just as an experiment.

SID: . . . suppose I just didn't have to be . . . I haven't figured out yet quite how I'm going to do it. I haven't been straight for like four years.

His spirits pick up momentarily at the thought of a new band, but in the end it's doom alone that counts.

SID: I had hepatitis and when I got out of the hospital I really fucked myself up as badly as I could. I don't know why but everybody said you can't do it, so I just went ahead and did it. It's my basic nature.

BAILEY: Your basic nature is going to get you in a lot of trouble.

SID: My basic nature is going to kill me in six months.

25

The Last Fuck You

THE SEX PISTOLS COMET, FRAGMENTING AS IT ENTERED THE earth's atmosphere, disintegrated on impact with the U.S.A. By the time most people heard of them they were history.

As the last shards of the Sex Pistols war wagon went up in flames there was great lamentation and gnashing of teeth, the ululations of the Tenaxed ones rising up in dingy clubs, sickness-unto-death spreading through suburban rec rooms.

I feel as if the bloody world has stopped turning.

Shirley X

Great Pan is dead! Here they were, the most famous band in the world and the deviant little buggers had to go and blow the bloody thing up. They blame each other, give contradictory stories to the press, but Lydon, McLaren, and Sid *wanted* (each for his own scaly reasons) to bring the House of Usher down upon their heads. If their original inspiration had been to smash the established order, equally seductive was the peevish fascination of self-annihilation.

Megalomaniacs all! Hell-bent on: self-immolation! petulant paroxysm! the frenzy of renown! crash and burn!

But to achieve a truly magnificent catastrophe you must first create an edifice worthy of your powers of devastation. Like children who through a long summer afternoon patiently build an elaborate sand castle with turrets and drawbridges and flags made of twigs and seaweed only to smash it to smithereens with ferocious glee and dance on the lumpy ruins.

How dare they! The little trolls wrecking their skanky creation! But—what else? Chaos was their mother, McLaren was their manager, outrage their modus operandi.

It was the nature of the beast. "It had to burn out," as Jah Wobble said; "it has the same energy of a four-year-old asserting itself on the world, when it throws a tantrum. It wasn't going anywhere else."

The Sex Pistols and their clamorous Svengali courted disaster on an operatic scale. Stuffing the Royals, terrorizing the land, turning the air blue. For their finale no common or garden-variety fuckup would do—it had to be of biblical proportions. They had attained such dark eminence that their own demise, for all intents and purposes, signaled the swan song of Punk rock as well. Winterland was the last fuck you. The Sex Pistols were the living embodiment of that fuck you. Which is why it made everybody so mad.

One night when no one was payin me any attention, an consumed wif angsty thoughts of the futility of life an that, I soliloquize to meself, "I fink I will end it all," an forthwith I hie meself to the bare bodkin. But lackin such I goes in the bathroom, breaks a glass an slashes me chest wif it. It's an excellent way to get sympathy—except wif them, a'course. They sez, "You botched it, you silly wanker! You did not carve yourself up realistic enough. You surely do not expect us to fall for amateur theatrics of that ilk. Better luck next time an you should arsk yer mum for some mecurachrome, that's a nasty scratch, that is, an it likely will come infected an you will die in agony heedlessly an wifout a fittin audience." Still an all I was quite pleased wif the results but shall endeavour to do a more professional job next time round.

Danny Fields (manager of the Ramones; scenemaker):

When the Sex Pistols broke up in San Francisco, it showed that the Punk thing wasn't viable. They were meant to self-destruct, and so what's the point in investing in any of them.

Punk barely a year old, in its most public phase, and dead in its tracks. *Après nous le déluge!*—or New Wave.

What could be more willful, more spiteful than to destroy your prize creation—a whole proto-civilization in miniature, really—just to show it's nothing to you. A fuckin' joke, man, a bloody piss-take is all it was. Even better, insist that it had been a big swindle all along. Far more impressive than just carrying on as if it were some frowsy little business.

Consequently the need—at least on the parts of Lydon and McLaren—to dismiss their creations. You've been had, mate. We leave Sid out of this. He had no wish to knock it; Sid was a true believer.

Lydon had been well bored with the charade for over a year now. He had become sullen and sour. The petulent narcissism of the prima donna had replaced the righteous anger of the dissenter. Even his apocalyptic pronouncements—"I want to just destroy everything!"—had taken on a tiresome predictability. He was bored. You wouldn't want Johnny to be bored now, would you? What would God do? He'd zimzum off into another universe. Probably become a noise structuralist.

As for McLaren, he was possessed by the schizophrenic motives of the impresario. Like the Who's maniacal manager, Kit Lambert, calamity, for McLaren, was almost preferable to success. It was more satisfying. More perverse. An ex-art student's infatuation with the shock tactics of modernism. C'mon now, any chartered accountant with a good Rolodex could manage a successful group, but creating a full-blown catastrophe was an art. Necessary, too, if he were to demonstrate the interchangability of the entities he managed. They were his creatures—clones with attitude—and he was free to dismiss them at will.

This, as nothing else could, would clearly demonstrate

170

that he alone was the source of an endless stream of wonders. I am the Great Oz, the *fons et origo* of all things.

Packing it in and on to the next hustle would reinforce his original premise that he could have done it with any likely bunch of yobs. If, as a manager, one were to make a huge success out of, say, Jimi Hendrix—what purpose would that serve? Any fool could do that. Far more impressive is the Tony Secunda approach to talent—serendipity: "I found the little wanker sitting under a tree in Hyde Park playing a guitar and I marched him into [name of record company withheld] next morning and got him a big fat three-record deal."

In Sid's case, his fetish for disaster—"me basic nature"— dominates everything. The genuine, if paranoid, pleasure of watching it all go utterly awry. He finds the mythology of self-destruction—the Iggytude of rock—irresistible. James Osterberg may be alive and well and living on the Lower East Side, Berlin, L.A.—wherever—but Iggy? Uh-uh. Sid didn't buy it. What did it matter what this Osterberg—Iggy's doppelgänger—did? Sid knew in his heart of hearts that Iggy committed suicide onstage nightly. Iggy, as no one else before him, was the living poltergeist of himself.

And Sid had every intention of following in his idol's footsteps.

26

Tin Men, Tin Gods

Our Foreign Correspondent Writes:

Top show biz moguls and TV personalities were convicted last week of eating Viciousburgers at New York's prestigious Studio 54 Disco in court hearing last week, after the latest of a series of Vice Squad raids on the "playground of the idle rich." . . . The last few years has seen an increase in this bizarre of vampirism, of which the Viciousburger is only the latest example. Vampires are noteworthy for consuming star corpses in the form of burgers in the mistaken belief that some of the star's charisma will rub off on them. This is just the latest example. . . . The cult is said to have begun in the fifties with Deanburgers.

—JAMIE REID COLLECTION, VICTORIA & ALBERT MUSEUM, LONDON.

THEY'D SET OUT TO REDEFINE ROCK 'N' ROLL, TO TAKE IT BACK from the Jimmy Pages and the Peter Framptons and redeem their brethren from the vinyl dark satanic mills. And, conceptually at least, they'd done it. "They moved rock to the limits of its form," says Lenny Kaye. *Well, wot more could you arsk?*

The battle for reality was over. They'd won! The hippie *reich* a frumpy joke, Clapton et al clobbered, the record companies a bloody laughingstock, and yet, and yet . . . While they were out there dancing on the tombs of the Boring Old Farts, the Imp of the Perverse played a trick on them.

173

They'd started out—barely more than a year ago—street-smart, abusively/dazzlingly articulate, shocking in a brutal/sexy way. Pied Pipers of all the little ghouls with bright red dyed hair and white faces with things stuck in their heads. Their fame spread like wildfire. National disgraces! International celebrities! Then—out of the blue—they were smitten with the seven plagues of Egypt. Fame, aloofness from fans, druggie-rock-star syndrome (Sid), fawning groupies, music-biz shenanigans, showboating, bodyguards. Their campaign against the wretched indulgences of rock stars had been so successful that they themselves were now rock stars. Just like, uh, Led Zeppelin, the Bee Gees, Peter Frampton, and the rest of the poxy scum. How vile. How *ironic*. How tedious.

"In America," said Steve Jones, "what fucked us up, is that they treated us like rock stars." Wot did you expect, mate? That *Billboard* create a new celebrity category for the Sex Pistols? Like, "Attitude Engineers," say, or "Punk Existentialists"? Tell us how you would like to be known, squire.

What were they thinking of? Did they really believe they were going to change the world? Very adolescent, that, to brood and curse because they'd failed in their bid for world domination. Thwarted in their mission they were now going to sulk, go off to Brazil, whine in grungy bars, shoot up and kill themselves.

You can't beat the system. Not Johnny Rotten with all his sarky, polyphrenic ranting, or Malcolm McLaren with his quest for existential ferocity. Whatever you did was not going to make a whole lot of difference to the blind, overarching forces of the entertainment biz. Successful musicians become rock stars. There is no way around this.

How could they have expected to maintain the pretense that they were just a bunch of Punk Everykids when for well over two years they'd been Punk royalty? Even at Club Louise as far back as the fall of 1976, when maybe a couple hundred people in all of London had ever heard of them, they were being fawned over and treated like Cockney nobility, and not by just any idle, gawking mob of gormless teens, but by future stars like Joe Strummer, Adam Ant, Siouxsie Sioux, Chrissie Hynde.

The Sex Pistols' renunciation of stardom had begun as an assault on the way audiences and performers related to each other. Subvert the passive state of reverie! That hypnotic thrall the spectator habitually falls under at rock concerts. In the old dispensation, fans were routinely seduced by the erotic ebb and flow between the band and themselves into something like a dream state.

Punk in its initial *putsch* attempted to thwart this cheesy trance state, violently shaking the audience out of its habitual torpor through abusive interaction and aggressive amateurism. Dispense with stage magic, pyrotechnics, guitar virtuosity! Along with such Tin Pan Alley flummery as hummable tunes and memorable lyrics. Was this the Great Work of rock—jingle fabrication, greeting-card sentiments?

It was a brilliant reversal but it couldn't last. This sort of experimental burlesque is only possible in a cult—fifty to a hundred faces. Once it escalates beyond the core group, it enters the media accelerator and becomes a metareligion.

ROTTEN (reading Rolling Stone): Wot, not bloody the Ramones, again? Five-towns slaggers wankin awf in the basement while Mum makes Fluffernutter sandwiches an Kool-Aid for lunch.

SID: Don' say such, John. It is from the Ramones I learnt everyfing I know. Dee Dee Ramone is me role model.

ROTTEN: I can well believe that an all. But "Sheena Is a Punk Rocker," I mean, really, get away!

SID: You have cited one a' me all-time favorites. Brilliant. Loik to see you do bettah!

ROTTEN: Still, on close examination, not wot I'd call one of the major ontological issues of our time, is it?

SID: Better'n workin as a fitter for the Durable Rubber Trolley Company, though, innit?

ROTTEN: I dunno, Sid-nay, is it?

SID: "Jesus loves you, life is rotten when the Lord is forgotten."

ROTTEN: Wot is that, a new composition of yours, Sidnay? About time you fuckin contributed to this stupid band.

SID: Nah, it's from a bleedin fundamentalist tract. Says 'ere that Rotten is as the antichrist—which I firmly believe. 'Ere. (Hands Rotten the pamphlet.)

"NO FUTURE FOR YOU!!!" So says Johnny Rotten, and it's not all lies—punk rock exposes the joke of man trying to save himself from the curse: "THE SOUL THAT SINS WILL SURELY DIE." TURN FROM YOUR PUNK WAYS an BE BAPTIZED INTO THE LIFE OF JESUS. . . .

Gobbing, insults, pogoing, casting yourself into the audience à la Iggy were ways around the chronic narcolepsy, but once you became famestruck—even infamous—there was little to be done. Denial only served to cast a spell all the more potent for not appearing to be there.

The current that flows between audience and performer is pure cosmic goo. Faith in human perfectibility and other such mass delusions being part of the consensual hallucination. The little guy up there from Slough, from Passaic, from some grubby little New Town. You may have worked at the supermarket checkout with the little fucker but once he's up there magnetizing the currents like Dr. Strange, he's no longer *that guy*, he's blown by solar winds, pulling in the future through the door with him.

With Cromwellian intolerance, Punk set out to abolish this quackery and along with it, rock 'n' roll's star system. The horrible plight that inevitably transformed the luminous raging street urchin with his Stratocaster into a Boring Old Fart cut off from his fans and surrounded by sycophants, bodyguards, and music-business functionaries. It had happened to all of them, one's cherished idols of childhood—Townshend, Jagger, Bowie. The only escape from this fate being to hang up your guitar, disband your group, and bail out. Even death wasn't a solution since death (especially a tragic, untimely death) would only feed rock's diabolic apparatus.

And what would be the point, except for the purposes of the publicist's handout, of claiming these beings are just like you and me? It would defeat the purpose of the thing. No amount of aloofness from scurvy music-biz manipulations, disdain for filthy lucre, contempt for the press, indifference to fame, would make a wick of difference. In the end all your Piety or Wit will not lure it back to cancel half a Line, nor all your Tears wash out a Word of it. It has all been foredained. IT IS WRITTEN, babe.

Take Pete Townshend and Jerry Garcia, both of whom at one time or another were revered as the "ideal rock star." These guys were compassionate, concerned, involved, (relatively) unassuming, ruthlessly self-examining—and look what happened to them. The unnatural effort involved in maintaining this schizophrenic state (God and Mr. Nice Guy) ended up wreaking havoc with Townshend's personal life and it as good as killed Garcia. And, after all was said and done, what did it amount to in the end? Goodwill, charitable acts, a bunch of soul-searching interviews in *Rolling Stone*.

This sort of well-intentioned interfering with the celestial clockwork of rock could well be construed as a form of self-congratulatory arrogance, the kind of brazen condescension that goes hand in hand with other such sixties effrontery as the campaigns to *transcend* rock (as envisioned by the Doors, the Who, the Grateful Dead). Sincere expressions of concern by the star for his fan is a mistake, sir, a self-ingratiating folly since it implies a wretched understanding of the nature of the beast.

To the fan, solicitousness on their behalf is simply ill-advised pettifoggery. Consideration for *us*? What is this shit? Immediately suspect.

Not only was the meddling of these do-goody busy-bodies another aberration of late-sixties presumptuousness, it was to have dire consequences. The demon doubt now entered the sacred precincts of rock. Skepticism became rampant and soon gave birth to that most corrosive of all heresies: rock criticism.

27

Is There Life After Sex Pistols?

SID RECOVERS, FLIES BACK TO LONDON TO REJOIN NANCY. THE Sex Pistols' notoriety was accelerated by their hit-and-run career, but its mana was fast evaporating. The power was draining out, but Sid, in his hallucinated parentheses of hubris and smack, was under the illusion that—just now—his power was coming on. An easy mistake to make at this point. It's early days yet.

Sid and Nancy are making plans, big plans. I mean, he's famous Sid, he's pure gold, isn't he? The world's his oyster. A bloody walking McLuhan epigram—infamous for being infamous, mate. Just add smack. *La vida es sueño, señor.*

Uncle Bill Burroughs would have diagnosed it *tout de*

suite, but Sid and Nancy are oblivious. The centipede sickness is something you don't see right away. The opiated Saragasso Sea—junk, downs, methadone—occludes all.

Meanwhile, in Rio, McLaren's recording Sid's "Belsen Was a Gas" with the train robber Ronnie Biggs and an American actor playing Martin Bormann in full Nazi regalia. But the farce has gone sour.

By the end of January, Lydon, Vicious, and McLaren are all back in England. There's not much sentiment about the demise of the Sex Pistols from any of them. "I'm so glad I'm out of that group," says Sid. "I won't work with any of them again," Lydon tells Caroline Coon. "And that's no great pity." McLaren is making similar noises, but he clearly cares a bit more than the other two, despite the fact that he'd all but engineered the breakup, counted on it *before* the American tour. He's planning—what else is new?—another Sex Pistols film, with or without Sex Pistols.

And you, being Sid Vicious, why should you care? You can always put another band together, can't you? Any bloody guitarist or drummer in the world would *kill* to be in that band, wouldn't they? Line forms to the left. *Beyond the Valley of the Sex Pistols.* Cover of the bleedin' *New Musical Express,* at least, mate. Might even make the front page of the *Sun.* SID VICIOUS FRONTING NEW GROUP! Well, it's *possible.* The thought of bigger and better things to come keeps the black dogs at bay.

Yeah, awright! Wasn't Sid indisputably *the* Sex Pistol? The American tour made that crystal-clear, didn't it? So . . . easy one. The most famous rocker in the world (me, isn't that right, Nance?) and a bunch of cool dudes. What could be simpler, mate? Just fink about it. But not too long.

But somehow it never gets together.

Hey, even his friend Lydon is talking about doing something with him. Forming a band. That slagging-Sid-off business is water under the bridge. You know Lydon, wind anybody up, he would, but all is forgotten now. Kiss and

Don't you fuckin say wot I fink you gonna say, either, ya tosser! It's 'cause I'm not ready, I 'aven't quite got me ducks in a row. The mix of personalities is the critical fing wif a band, now, innit?

make up. But guess what? That doesn't happen either.

McLaren still fiddling about with his Punkumentary. Where are we now, film number 4, number 5? He'll paste it all together, make it end up looking the way he wants it, minus Lydon. Fuck Lydon! Lydon would never have cooperated anyway. He has his own theories, his own agenda, which interfered with everything. He would have got in the way. McLaren began as a *bricoleur*, his student film was a psycho-geographical montage. And that's what he still was in essence, a piecer-together of stuff. Now he would splice the Sex Pistols back together again. Reassemble the parts in any order you like and make it look as if that was the way you meant to do it all along.

Lydon felt McLaren had stolen his soul, and so (perhaps

out of spite, necessity, or disillusion—whatever) he was gone and he wasn't coming back for any poncey documentary or any amount of lolly, either. So much the better, muses McLaren. He'll make Sid the Sex Pistols' protagonist, the real icon of the group. Besides he is more impressionable, more pliable than Lydon.

Sid Vicious was McLaren and Westwood's favorite child. "He would do anything that John wouldn't do," says Julien Temple. "He was more malleable as a Sex Pistol, but he hated Malcolm with a vengeance. Malcolm couldn't control John intellectually, but he could control Sid, although not physically, or as a junkie. When Sid became a junkie, it was all over."

28
My Way

Four Stars Are Born, with Julien Temple as director. McLaren takes Sid to Paris to construct the central sequence around him. Sid is all that he has left of the Pistols at this point. The scenario would be a metaphor for the whole Sex Pistols farrago, up to and including their decline and fall. A fall from grace, that. The Pistols' slide into acceptance being in McLaren's eyes their downfall.

To show this, the audience would have to be very respectable and middle-class. The French bourgeoisie would be perfect stooges, the very epitome of conventional taste. And then he'd have Sid sing some blowsy old frog torch song expressing defiance and existential ennui. A Punk Piaf, how droll! An excellent plan but just try to get Sid to sing "Je ne regrette rien." Good luck.

Things aren't going too well at the rehearsals, and back at the Hotel Brighton McLaren is fuming. From his bed he calls Sid's room and like an enraged Diaghelev taunts him over the phone: "You're a fucked-up junkie. You're worthless. You're washed up, a fuckin' sick joke." On and onandon he goes. While McLaren is screaming with pique and frustration—his toy is broken, the circuits are jammed—Sid gives the phone to Nancy while he hightails it up to McLaren's room. McLaren keeps ranting on to Nancy and—suddenly—the door of this eighteenth-century room in the Hotel Brighton on the Rue de Rivoli is kicked open and there's Sid in his motorbike boots and swastika underpants. He's consumed with impotent rage at McLaren. He jumps on him, kicks him, punches him. McLaren runs out of the room and along the corridor with all the laundry women saying, *"Oh, monsieur! Monsieur!"*

At that instant it all came out, all the accumulated bile. Sid felt betrayed, abandoned. The rage at being deceived, denied his fifteen minutes, his dream stolen.

Julien Temple:

He was totally infested with a kind of rock 'n' roll tradition by then, through Nancy and through the Heartbreakers, and his big gripe was that Malcolm would never let them play and never be a rock 'n' roll group, which Sid really wanted to be, I think.

So, a new plan is made, a *better* plan, really. *Sid Sings Sinatra*. "My Way" being the American version of "Je ne regrette rien," after all. Brilliant. Wif Sid mockin' Ol' Blue Eyes, sending up the old lounge lizard's jaded croak. A merciless burnt-out parody is the idea, demolishing the most narcissistic song of all time—that would be just the ticket. Sid as Sinatra. But Sid nixes this. He's got a better idea, yet. He wants to do it like the Ramones! The Ramones as Sinatra. Now this is hip. So he does the first verse as a goofy Sinatra, or, really, *Goofy Sings Sinatra*, and then lurches into Ramones bamalama.

Temple:

He had great intuition about cameras. Sid was the Sex Pistols because he was their number one fan, and that was the greatest thing about having him in the group. Sid was getting demoralized because the dream was broken. Not only the dream of being a pop star, but this thing with which he was in love as a fan, as a guy at the 100 Club with or without a beer glass. That was his PR. Rather than the group dying, the audience dies. He loved the idea of shooting the audience: We wanted him to shoot his mother. We saw Sid as the first monster child of the hippie generation.

He's sweating, he can't remember the words, he's having trouble. But he *looks* perfect. The image is down cold.

He's just a little disoriented—the Sid-on-Sid effect is a little dizzy-making. Nancy rewrites the words for him and what he can't remember he makes up. *"I strangled a cat, I did this and that."*

Okay we're ready to shoot. Lights, action. . . . Sid, or Gary Oldman as Sid—the Punk immaculate, sidling insolently down that Hollywood-musical staircase, a gauzy dream set originally built for Serge Gainsborg. Sid in a distressed dinner jacket and motorcycle boots, skinny, all in black spiky hair. Punk descending a staircase, as if the steps themselves were made of light, walking down this kitsch Jacob's ladder from star heaven to the groundling fan-pit beneath.

As Sid sings "My Way," while shooting the audience, fan and star are in a kind of dream state, the quintessential episode where fan and star fuse into one another in an facsimile *liebestod*. Like Danton's severed head signing the *Marseillaise* in an empty room, Sid at that moment is the solipsistic star performing for his ideal audience, himself.

Here—materialized—the tidal current between star and fan—the very essence of the thing! Chakra snakes of the Unseen Being! That synaptic leap! Wave or particle? Bothatonce! Oceanic state! Orgasmic instant! That moment when . . . star + fan = Other.

This was the genius of Sid. He *knew*—in his bones—did Sid. This was mother's milk to him, he was an expert on this schizy stuff. Star-fetishism was what Sid and McLaren had in common. Neither of them had any interest in dismantling the star system or any of those situationist shibboleths. To actually disown the personality cult as prescribed by killjoy philosophes—out of the question, mate. It would have defeated the whole purpose of the thing. Eliminated him. You can't have an impresario without stars.

The others had bemoaned their fate during the U.S. tour—this bothersome rock-star business that had been thrust upon them. Not Sid of course. As the personification of the ultimate fan he knew that this was nonsense, highfalutin talk from a bunch of jumped-up barrow boys. This star business wasn't something you wanted to be coy about. Especially from a mob of them liggers, slaggers, wankers, pseudos, tea leafs, and talented layabouts—what were they complaining about? They were lucky to *be* fuckin' stars. What was all this quasi-ideological breast-beating about the inequitable relationship between audience and performer? Maybe the fans *liked* it that way, did you ever think of that, John Lydon?

Sid understands the Lowly Worm syndrome of the fan only too well. Yer basic fan, far from wanting stars to be just like them—why would I want to idolize someone just like me?—*demands* insolence, megalomania from their idols—veritable Assyrian personalities who peer down on him from a great height. This is all we ask from rock stars, really, that they *don't* behave like us, and that would pretty much entail the usual gamut of wretched excess: reckless, irrational, self-destructive behavior—whatever. We paid good money! Bring on the kamikazes! We want to see it all—mindless destruction, overweening insolence, boorish narcissism—people misbehaving *very* badly. The star has an obligation, he's required by papal fiat to drive cars into swimming pools. Trash motel rooms, throw the TV out the window. Demolish Holiday Inns and generally carry on in the despotic Persian manner. It's his job.

Tin gods! That's what we come to see. Without that essential abasement, how are we to achieve our collective orgasm, the buzz of the *ummah*, the tribal hive—endorphins streaming through the brain like tiny lunatic surfing gods?

Sid wasn't one to disappoint. "I'm the only one putting real energy into it," he complained on the American tour. Aside from the sarky abuse (which by now he could do in his sleep), what was Rotten contributing? Did he mutilate himself, bash fans with his bass, perform fellatio onstage?

Shirley X with her x-ray specs saw it, saw through all the flimflam, fan radar burning through the smokescreen:

> I honestly think Johnny changed more than anyone
> else. I mean, well, this bodyguard business shows
> that he was the one turning himself into a rich, im-
> portant star, and I've loved the Pistols since he was
> a cheeky bugger that swore at Bill Grundy. That's
> the way I like Johnny, arrogant with his fixed opin-
> ion, but these days he is polite-spoken and he talks
> a load of rubbish.

While Rotten was busy deconstructing the star, Sid wanted only to bring it to spectral perfection. He was a Kabuki actor who stepped over the line, gone mad somewhere between the theater and the street. The doomed flight of Icarus, Kerouac's roman candles. A hysterical stereotype it may be, but if the stars are to stay in their courses, if stadiums are to be filled, the cannibal god must be appeased. Pounding hearts must be ripped from the breasts of sacrificial victims. And Sid was nothing if not a willing victim.

29
The Afterlife

REWIND TO JANUARY 17, 1978. THE PHONE CONVERSATION WITH
Roberta Bailey. Sid, the vatic Punk, is predicting the future
of his mates from his hospital bed: "I dunno, they'll probably try and get another band together and fail. John is completely finished." It's a premonition, all right, but not about
John Lydon. Lydon will always land on his feet, the other two,
Cook and Jones, can take care of themselves. But Sid, outside the context of the Pistols, is a comic, pathetic figure
rapidly approaching the vanishing point. It's Sid who is finished, and hasn't yet heard the news. He never will. It's all
over for him except the shouting. The devils are already

sharpening their pitchforks. Sid is theirs; it's only a matter of time.

Sid and Nancy hole up for a while in Pindock Mews in Maida Vale, London's drugs central. Run sequence from Lech Kowalski's Sex Pistols documentary, *D.O.A.:*

> Sid and Nancy lying in bed, stoned, trying to do an interview. Sid nodding out, Nancy prodding him awake. At one point he burns Nancy with a cigarette. He plays with a large hunting knife, like some ominous stage prop you know is going to get used in the third act. "Sid and Nancy," she dreamily declares, "we were partners in crime, we helped each other out."

30

Flashback

REWIND TO SUNDAY, APRIL 3, 1977. HE HAS JOINED FORCES with an even more zealous fan than himself—if that were possible. His romance with Nancy Spungen and his becoming a rock star combined with the Oklahoma death trip of rock are all now hopelessly intertwined. A Gorgon's head of lethal serpents that no mirror will dispel.

They'd met the day he officially became a Sex Pistol. She'd come to London when the Heartbreakers came over. She was looking for Jerry Nolan, the Heartbreakers' drummer, when they ran into one another. At first she set her sights on Johnny Rotten, and when he'd have nothing to do with her she attached herself to Sid. Permanently.

He was a Punk star, she an enterprising haute groupie with some nasty habits. It was hardly an accidental meeting. Once he was in the group, it was like, "Oo-er, never thought it was going to be like this, where's the chicks?" And what kind of chicks do rock stars meet? Groupies. And now they want to complain about her? That some scene-making groupie stole their Sidney away? She gave him sex and a drug habit. He wanted nothing less. He was a crash dummy with a crash dummy's name, and heading straight for that brick wall anyway. Who was looking out for him? Not Lydon or Westwood or McLaren. Without her he would have been more lost than he already was. He was barely mature sexually. She was—out of the blue—his dream girl, a CBGB Daisy Mae on hard drugs.

Nancy:

We slept in the same bed for five nights before we screwed. We screwed as a joke, really. He didn't appeal to me sexually then. One night I woke up and he was rubbing up and down against my thigh and I said: "Sid, what do you think you're doing?" He said to me: "How is it that the birds I fancy never like me?" So the next night we were down at the Roxy. I said to him, right, tonight we'll go home and screw. And we went home and we did. We did it in the bedroom, we did it in the bathroom, we did it everywhere.

On the first night we screwed he had smelly feet and he wet the bed.

I find him sexually attractive now. Don't you think he has a sexual aura? I've taught him everything he needs to know. I've put that sexual aura into Sid, he was pretty near a virgin before. He was turned on by me like he never was before. He had a schoolboy crush on me. You know people say that I've grown up too fast. Well maybe that's true but I think I've grown up pretty damn smart.

The standard line on Nancy is that she was a ruthless, rapacious scene-making junkie prostitute. A *New York* scene-making junkie prostitute. A chick so low she'd fuck guys for drugs. Or procure drugs for stars so they'd sleep with her. A clued-in broad who clearly knew the backstage rates-of-exchange. Getting rock stars drugs so they'll look kindly on you is an ancient, time-worn tradition. Deejays do it, even educated fleas do it. Sex and drugs, mama, these are the whirring dream-engines that drive rock—and basketball. Sex was her job, stupid. She was good at it.

Most of this Nancy-bashing you have to put down to the endemic misogyny of the rock scene, which is only marginally tempered by Punk's allegedly unisex ethos. *Hey, we allowed chicks to be in bands, didn't we?*

As if, somehow, she'd gotten it all wrong. C'mon, when you're flaunting Third Reich regalia, Charles Manson mutilation-redemption fantasies, and Sacher Masoch rubber underpants—what did you expect, the dialectics of nihilism? It's a little late to start saying, oh, you got us all wrong, we never intended to encourage self-destructive behavior. *It was all, you know, ironical, mate.*

You can't expect everybody to tune in to the postmodern equivocal ideology of it all. It's all very well for those cerebral dabblers down the King's Road, diddling with transparent countercultural subtexts and claiming it's all a put-on, darling, a big ontological joke. There were bound to be those who were too far gone to slip comfortably back into paradoxical bed-sits, who would take it all at face value. Even their little protégé, Sid, had by this point forgotten the Vicious business was a joke. What begins as farce ends as tragedy.

Pictures of Sid and Nancy at the arraignment (a fresh angle for the tabloid feeding-frenzy, this): SEX PISTOL SID VICIOUS HAS VIOLENT, DRUG-RELATED ROMANCE WITH JUNKIE PROSTITUTE. PICTURES ON PAGE 3. Turn to page 3. And there he is, Sid, pale and cadaverous with drooping eye and malevolent expression, her rock fantasy come true. And Nancy strutting her stuff in stiletto-heeled boots, a mop of wild, white hair, and defiant pout. Wot a fuckin' pair! Punk couple of the year, those two. The Arnolfinis of 1978, veritably.

Still, it may be technically inaccurate to describe Nancy, as many did, as a mere groupie. She would've vehemently denied it. As if appearing before some congressional subcommittee she swore on oath: "I am not or never have been a groupie. If a groupie came up to Sid, he'd kick her in the face."

She was a professional, a sex worker by trade. A dominatrix in an S&M club, beating German bankers for money, making them crawl on the floor and lick her boots. Mistress Grimhelda's, where Punk fashion seamlessly intersects with the kinky sex trade. Black leather garters, boots with nine-inch heels—she didn't even have to change clothes to go to work. A junkie punkette prostitute punishing the captains of industry—a bit of New Wave irony for you.

Home movie: The Spungens, a nice middle-class Jewish family living in suburban Philadelphia. Their first child, Nancy, is born. The new baby is doted on by her mother, Debbie. They are a close, loving family. But at some point the picture darkens, odd things start to happen. The Partridge Family scenario is mutating into a horror movie. There is something wrong with the baby girl, very wrong. She cries incessantly day and night as if a changeling, a demon child. Nothing seems to be wrong with her physically, no one can explain it. She is so disturbed that at age three psychiatrists are called in but no cause is ever found for the unremitting anguish that torments her. Her favorite holiday is Halloween. As a teenager she is irresistibly drawn to drugs. Pot, speed, downs, coke. The usual adolescent pharmacopeia. But it goes a little

OI, NANCE, YOU GOTTA PASTE THIS ONE IN THE SCRAPBOOK. LISSEN'A THIS: "LORRY DRIVER, JAMES HOLMES, FORTY-SEVEN, WAS OUTRAGED THAT HIS EIGHT-YEAR-OLD SON LEE HEARD THE SWEARIN AN KICKED IN THE SCREEN OF HIS TV. 'I BLEW IT UP, AN I WAS KNOCKED BACKWARD. I WAS SO ANGRY AN DISGUSTED WITH THIS FILTH THAT I TOOK A SWING WITH MY BOOT.'" JAMES HOLMES, A MAN OF PRINCIPLE. I LIKE THAT.

bit further than that. Her friend Karen tries to talk her out of shooting speed—You'll kill yourself—but it's the wrong approach. She *wants* to kill herself.

By January 1975 she's found her zone, punk rock. Becomes a go-go dancer. Track marks on the insides of her elbows, on the back of her hands. Heroin locks Nancy, as it would Sid, into permanent adolescence.

She is smart, she is with-it, she knows everyone on the scene and she doesn't give a damn what they think; they can hate her guts if they want. Nothing is going to deter her from her appointed rounds, she is one determined girl. She can be tough as nails, but her daydream is a gauzy fantasy. Punk Barbie. She recounts her idea of bliss with the dewy revery of a Judy Blume heroine on smack:

> It's just that ever since I've gone out with guys, I've gone out with musicians. . . . The most exciting things started to happen around 1975. But I wasn't really concentrating on the punk scene. I was concentrating on big rock 'n' roll stars like Ron Wood and Mick Jagger—I know him but I never fucked him. I was with Keith Richards. I toured around with Aerosmith for a while.
>
> I had a good time, and I got treated nice, you know? It was the fun of it. It was exciting. I'm friends with just about everybody. Musicians—a lot of them are really nice, you know?
>
> But sometimes they are really terrible.

I mean what would Punk heaven *be?* You are in the stretch limo with Whatisname. Full bar, anything you want, darling, just name your poison. MTV pulsating, sound off, stereo blasting the little tin god's latest mix. Me vocals a little too far down in the track, don'tcha think, Chas? Smokin' hash, drinkin' Remy in fuckin' huge tumblers, man, a couple

> **NOTE TO SELF: MAKE APPOINTMENT FOR NANCY WIF PLASTIC SURGEON. GET BIRTHMARK OFF HER ARSE SO AS SHE CAN PURSUE HER CAREER AS A STRIPPER WIFOUT HINDRANCE.**

of rails of dynamite blow. What do you care of Spanish or Russian politics?

To Nancy there is no person on earth more desirable than a rock star, and at this juncture of the planets, Punk is ascendant. The hippest, most obnoxious form of the rock virus yet to come down the pike. Getting Sid as a boyfriend, *your* boyfriend, right at this moment, year of our Lord 1977, is a consummation devoutly to be wished. The equivalent of, say, Anita Pallenberg snagging Keith Richards circa spring of 1967.

But it's something of a fatal attraction. She triggers in him a self-destructive impulse he hadn't previously exhibited. According to his mum: "He latched into hers. If there was two people in the whole goddamn world who should never ever met it was those two. People liken them to Romeo and Juliet. It was an absolute tragedy. But they did, and meeting, met self-destruction."

What did he see in her, you say, this cheeseball that they all hated, even the girls, even Chrissie Hynde? But then she was almost Mrs. Vicious once (for visa purposes only, of course). But darling, it's not *your* romance, of course you don't get it. Nobody did, practically. You're not meant to. Cue Elvis: "That's When Your Heartaches Begin." It's mad love, *amour fou*, Punk love, junk love. You're spending the weekend at some filthy-rich A&R guy's beach house in Malibu and some jerk has just run into the room shouting, "Vesuvius is erupting! You gotta get outta here *right now*!" Burning ash forming on the rooftops, molten lava not more than half a mile off, incinerating everything—downtown Los Angeles a mangled heap of stucco and neon—but you don't care. Let it come!

He's in love, she's the most beautiful thing he's ever seen, a bona fide Punk goddess. As for Nancy, she thinks she's died and gone to heaven. Sid fuckin' Vicious, man! *Hers.* They're smitten. You can't argue with this kind of thing.

Powdery mounds of pumice piling up against the windowpanes, people screaming in the streets, but you, the undead, in the House of the Carbonized Credenza, are past caring. As if the frames are flickering past in the light of a firestorm, Poly Styrene watches Sid, catatonic at John's house, playing with his big knife, and talks of him as if about a ghost: "He was gone: it was quite a hellish planet."

August. Late afternoon. Sid and Nancy are passed out on a grungy mattress. Their friend, John Shepperton, is in bed with them—dead some eight hours from a cocaine overdose. After twenty minutes of trying to wake the dead, Sid and Nancy realize they've spent the night with a corpse. Wot the fuck!

Sid and Nancy move temporarily into Gunther Grove with Lydon, but by the end of August, they have overstayed their welcome. Losing their keys, turning up in the early hours of the morning, kicking the door in. Enough is enough, and eventually another enraged houseguest woken up too many mornings by the Demented Duo attacks them with an ax! Nancy hides her black eye behind sunglasses, but Sid takes this as the final blow. They decide to go to New York. *Big* mistake.

> **You'll look in vain for yer diminished sevenths wif me. None of yer Jack Bruce paradidlin Coltrane-solos-on-your-fretless-bass nonsense wif this lad. Just yer pure existential essence, if I do say so meself. I sing the solid body electric. Me mere presence speaks volumes. This is why Rotten calls me the philosopher of the group. An it ain't on account of me skill as a phenomenologist that 'ee sez that, a'course not. Excuse the vainglorious revel but I is philosophy in motion. None of your fogyish explication need apply 'ere, ol' son. Let's face it, fashion is far more ontological than any bloody silly axiom, innit? I writes in me diary on this glorious day: "The monster 'as taken over an ate itself." Wise words, indeed, but wot the fuckin 'ell it means is your guess as good as mine. A surfeit of sulfate I should fink. An so to bed.**

To raise some money, Sid and Nancy front a concert at the Electric Ballroom in Camden as the Vicious White Kids— Steve New, Rat Scabies, and Glen Matlock. The following day they leave for New York.

31
The Afterlife Reinvented

LIKE COUNTLESS OTHERS—GIVE ME YOUR TIRED, YOUR WEARY, your Punks, your junkies—they had come to the States to start a new life. They would get off drugs. Nancy would manage Sid. They might even get married. Their first week there Sid collapses in the lobby of the Chelsea Hotel. Not a good start.

But if London was hostile, New York is worse. There are a lot of bitter, belligerent people on the scene who are less than thrilled with a burned-out Sex Pistol and his moll in their midst. The Sex Pistols and their manager had stolen the CBGB scene lock, stock, and barrel. Stolen Richard Hell's head (and the contents thereof), stolen the basic uniform (even the safety-pin mania began in New York)—they'd even run off with *the name itself* and made it theirs. And when the New York punks pitifully complained, "Hey, get your grubby, limey hands off; this movement's already taken!" The Brits came back with: "Oh, you wouldn't understand. Punk started in England. You know, everyone is on the dole there. Punk is really about class warfare and economic blah, blah, blah." Then, to top it all off, after stealing the sacred fire, the Brits had bombed it into the ground.

Sid in New York makes an ideal scapegoat. Once outside the charmed circle of the Sex Pistols, he is exposed, a victim, vulnerable to all the hostility and envy that is out there toward the Sex Pistols. He's an easy target, someone you could wind up just by looking at him. Any opportunity to bash the little fucker verbally or otherwise.

Imprisoned by his past, his image larger than life, he begins issuing ludicrous challenges to assorted Punks: "So you're Jeff Magnum/Stiv Bators/Eliot Kidd. You think you can beat me up?"

When he plays Max's in early September, many come expecting to see the rabid star of the infamous Sex Pistols tour. What they get is a weedy ectomorph with skull-like head and protruding paunch, someone old before his time, nodding through several Punk archetypes. He collapses several times during the set and Nancy has to yank him back up onto his feet. He ends up slithering across the floor like a snake. They are stunned. *This* is Sid Vicious? Once he'd known how to put on a good horrorshow, allright, but junk turned Sid into a droid. He had even forgotten how to play *himself*. Half the audience could have done a better Sid.

32

A Punk in New York

> **Doin cold turkey in the lobby an wot's this? The fuckin plastic rubber plant's comin to life! I swear to keep meself from temptation from this day forth, holy chrikey! Polyester caterpillars crawlin thru me brain. It's that syphilitic hairy green wallpaper wot's done it! Keep off me, ya slimy li'l bastards! I fink I just 'eard Poly Styrene singin "X-rays penetrating thru the latex breeze." Probably just a faulty air-conditionin' unit communin wif itself. But wot fresh 'ell is this? ENUF, YOU FUCKIN FIENDS! If I hear Debby Boone sing "You Light Up My Life" one more time I'm gonna puke.**

DAILY INCIDENTS AT THE SPRING STREET METHADONE CLINIC. Taunted and provoked by other addicts, he gets into fights. *He's got this hot button, mum, and they just won't leave it alone.* Goes out less and less. Nods off in the bed with a lit cigarette, sets the mattress on fire. They get moved to the infamous room 100 on junkie row. Lights out, shades drawn, take-out food containers, soda cans, dirty laundry. Frustration, impotent rage, flare ups. Still capable of hair-raising acts of passion. Dangling Nancy out of the window, beating her up, biting her ear off. When he breaks her nose, punches her out, it's usually over drugs. Love stinks.

Still, this is the life, ain't it? This is the way rock stars live. Hendrix, Keith Richards—the sunshine bored the day-lights out of them, too. Heavy curtains over the windows. Dracula sleeping in his coffin. So be it.

Lydon:

Sid was one of the major gullible's travels. Sid couldn't see that it was just a sham and an image. To Sid, that was the way New York stars lived their lives morning, noon and night. He thought they all went to bed with their high heels on.

Unremitting fatalism hovers over all. They're in the doldrums. Ruthless failure, so unrelenting it seems intentional, undoes any possible escape. Even when that redeeming glimmer of light appears, the Max's Kansas City gigs, you make sure you fuck it up. Like falling down a mineshaft day after day. Nancy *was* obnoxious, but many of the people she pissed off deserved it. Her insufferable attitude was just a form of aggressive high-strung touchiness, done out of desperation and junkie coo-coo cloudland megalomania. The Punk pond was already an inflated you-are-if-you-think-you-are kingdom where it was all pretty much your perception. Who's to say who rates at the LCD Club; who's more important than you, anyway? Who is to say what sort of sense of our own importance would be delusional down here at the Terminal Hotel? Just add a few rails of coke.

"Hey, muthafucka! This is Sid fuckin' Vicious we're talking about. Fuck you! You ought to be licking his boots, schmuck! Hey, man, you know I didn't mean it, c'mon. Got a ten-spot you can spare? Give you head in the john if you'll help us out just this once."

But beyond all the bluster they must have seen the picture was breaking up, the *malabolge* twinkling below. Room 100 was perched, teetering on the ledge, right over that infernal pit—they lived right above it!—the eighth circle of hell boiling up, the snapping fish calling to them all night long. The discount carpet emporium across Twenty-third Street is flashing cryptic messages: I GO ON EXISTING LIKE BASALT! . . . HOW LONG HAS IT BEEN SINCE I RESEMBLED MYSELF? When you start getting neon communiqués from the Tomb of the Unknown Punk, you know it's only a matter of time.

Sid and Nancy spend a weekend at Nancy's parents' house outside Philadelphia (recounted in Deborah Spungen's book, *And I Don't Want to Live This Life*, and re-created in *Sid and Nancy*). The farcical nature of this encounter is not due to a clash of hipsters and squares. It's the utter out-of-itness and lostness of the two Punk waifs that is both comic and poignant.

Of the Spungens' brick-faced, aluminum-sided tract-house colonial, Sid hilariously gasps: "It's a fucking palace." Ditto the steak-and-corn-on-the-cob dinner on the patio. "Best fuckin' food I ever ate."

They retire to the den to hear Sid play. According to Nancy's mum, "Sid proceeded to bang out two chords, clumsily and with great difficulty. Then he stopped and looked up, grinning crookedly. That was it, that was what he wanted to show us."

In bed, back at the Chelsea, naked, watching Saturday-morning cartoons. Take a swig of methadone from the Fairy Lotion bottle. Feet hit the street. The past looms up. Nancy has a scrapbook with all the newspaper photos and stories about herself and Sid, including the busts. Sid is infamous but it's a pluperfect form of fame—all in the past tense. What good did it do, anyway, his fame, his infamy, without substance? It was a blind alley. Sinking slowly into their own anecdotage. He was now unreachable, smack reinforcing his fixations, sealing him in a tomb of his own fictions.

Morbidity sets in. Sid was in love with the mythology of self-destruction. "Desperate to get into anything that would kill him," said his mate Lydon. But repetition, like a spell uttered too many times, was materializing his doomsday. "Sid always used to say he didn't want to live past twenty-one," says Wobble. "Often people talk that way, it's the old James Dean thing, but when you assume something, you can become it, and it becomes dangerous."

Sid's fatalistic declarations about his imminent demise were always tinged with bravado. Perhaps there was even a cry for help in them, but Nancy's were adamantine, there wasn't a shred of self-pity in them. It was a clear-eyed headlong plunge into the abyss.

Debbie Spungen:

We drove in silence for a while. And then out of nowhere, Nancy quietly said, "I'm going to die very soon. Before my twenty-first birthday. I won't live to be twenty-one. I'm never gonna be old. I don't wanna ever be ugly and old. I'm an old lady now, anyhow. I'm eighty. There's nothing left. I've already lived a whole lifetime. I'm going out. In a blaze of glory."

Avenue B and 2nd Street. Out on the street they're hawking brands. Toilet! General Westmoreland! Krang! A yellow line painted around the block steers customers to the dealer's den. B-boys and wild-style writers, tagburners.

Abandoned building. Filing up the stairs, total darkness, a great long line of junkies, very quiet. You almost wouldn't know they're there. Nervous silence. A scene from Dante or Celine. Morose, imploded. When you get up there, there's two slots in a steel door where you put your money through. *C* for cocaine, *H* for heroin. Like some mystic pharmacological temple where you pay tribute to the god of Nod. There's no deals down there on Avenue B. But Sid thinks he can bargain! He's demanding a special rate. On account of, y'know, him being him and all that. The jerk is so out of it.

Remember what Uncle Bill Burroughs always said: Dope is the ultimate product. The customer will kill to get it.

Shoot up and you're back there, in the zone. You're Sid Vicious, you're a star. *I am the most famous rock star in the world and that's the god's honest truth, innit? Who, if not me?* All the noisome little boxes snapping shut. Those clamorous little boxes that say, "You're fucked up, man, you're a useless piece of shit, muthafucka. You're a has-been. Sid fuckin' Useless should be your name." All the gibes, all the insults, the abusive lip-music from the methadone-clinic junkies, all silenced. A great, humming, warm cocoon, amniotic flow. Smack insulates the dream. In there it's all right. Food of the gods. Life is simple, all you gotta do is score. Nancy, ya fucking slut, go out and score me some more amniotic sea, bitch!

Functioning (barely) under a cloud of junk and methadone. He totters, he doesn't remember—who else was there? Where am I? The condition he's in, he hasn't got a clue. A loose cannon rolling down the grassy knoll and he's dragging the whole Punk doom train down with him. Disillusioned? We're all fucking disillusioned.

Smack is a way of readjusting the picture without changing the channel. You can tell yourself anything, anything imaginable, and you'll buy it. Guaranteed, or your money back. "It was a logical way for Punk to go," says Al McDowell. "Junk is a drug which is absolutely right for those aging rockers, it's the only way to make you think you're still great."

Staggering, spinning like a leaf in the wind. Conditions are not improving, in fact it's all going down the drain. Rapidly. Now even *they* can see they're fucked, that this is terminal. A bit too terminal. More and more frequently the cathode-ray tube is pulsating: THE END, THE END, THE END, and it ain't in Vulcanian hieroglyphs anymore. We're going off the air. The star-spangled banner, shots of plane formations. A flag waving like a detached hand. Where? Iwo Jima House of Pancakes, Roto-Rooter Six Flags Adventure. So . . . the last refuge of the junkie . . . We'll clean up. Sure. No, I really mean it this time. Yeah, that's it! That's what we'll do. Brilliant, Nance!

But hell, we're too fucked up, and anyway, calling in our state, we're never gonna get into a decent rehab. Your mom could call! Good old Debbie. He loved Debbie. He loves *his* mom too, but he's adopted Debbie—like his mom, Ma Vicious, but more together. A mom like you see in sitcoms, in the movies. Nancy calls her mom, Debbie calls the clinic, it's almost set up. Ready to go. Well, it's possible, isn't it? It *could* happen. Any other time we'd just wait around and see if the Terrible Twosome actually get it together. *Sid and Nancy Go to Rehab*. But, alas, tonight happens to be *that* night.

A party over at Sid's place. Room 100, Chelsea Hotel, Twenty-third Street between Seventh and Eighth. A bunch of rock peripheria, lowlifes, and druggies drifting in and out. Ten, twelve people hanging out. Little side deals going on, no chairs, nowhere to sit but on the bed and that's taken. Sid's not going to be much fun, he's already crashed out on twenty Tuinals. Nancy talking, doing her Cockney accent, Mrs. Vicious Punk hostess.

New York Post October 13, 1978

SID VICIOUS SEIZED AT CHELSEA HOTEL
Punk Rock Star Accused of Slaying Girlfriend.
His face pale and scratched, the dazed-looking Vicious muttered curses and "I'll smash your cameras," as he was led from the hotel, when the body of Nancy Laura Spungen, 20, clad in blood-soaked black lace bra and panties, was found crumbled under the bathroom sink.

Each story more plausible than the next. *Rashomon* in the Chelsea Hotel. What happened? Chaos, confused states, a farrago of stage doors, seedy types, rock lowlifes, and drug deals. Polypharmacy, robbery, murder. Or was it a botched suicide pact?

Sid confesses to photographer Joe Stevens:

> She smacked me on the nose just where I'd been punched [by the bellhop] and I took the knife out and said: "Do that again, I'm going to take your fucking head off." And she stuck her belly right in front of my knife. She didn't know. I didn't know we'd done anything really bad. She crashed out on the bed. I crashed out on the other. I woke up first and decided to get some methadone. Took a forty-five-minute taxi ride.

So that's it, he did it. He's admitted it. A bona fide confession. But wait a minute. The story he's telling, it's almost *too* coherent. Too pat. Wouldn't Lieutenant Columbo want to poke around a bit, lift a few corners? How did it all fit together so neatly, given the morass of altered states and tangled intentions? Especially in the narcoticized state he was in. Behind twenty Tuinals and a cup of methadone, you aren't going to remember the scene in too much detail. Even *un*medicated life isn't like that. It's flashes, disconnected incidents.

Anyway, Sid believes he's a dirty dog and so naturally he

blames himself. Even if he didn't do it, he was there, he didn't prevent it. He *could* have done it, he *wanted* to do it. Christ, she even asked him to do it. Many times. He's sentencing himself in the court of mea culpa, ridding society of this menace—himself. Mutatis mutandis he's guilty as sin, monstrously guilty. Inadvertently, out of carelessness, killed his other self.

Also, it's embarrassing. Whether you did it or not. Embarrassing not to remember what happened, to be woken up incoherent and your girlfriend dead. Even more embarrassing for a true believer of Punk to deny having done it. After all that tough talk and Dirty Harry posturing.

His added explanation is to say he as good as killed her. But this, from Sid Vicious, sounds too absolving, abstract, like some whiny rationalization. Far better just to say: I did it. Anyway, he figures, maybe he did do it. Sure, I probably did! Listen buster, *Sid Vicious* would be capable of this—*way!*

And from there it's just a short step to connecting all the pieces and putting them—and the overwhelming guilt—into a coherent story. *How I Did It. How Sid Killed Nancy. Sid's Story.* It's believable enough, no question about that. No one's gonna argue with him on this one. It works. It's like writing the lyrics to a song. When it hangs together, you've nailed it. Not that he did *that* too often.

Nancy's mom, Debbie Spungen, has a theory (and it's actually Sid's mom's theory too) that it was a botched suicide attempt. In an overarching psycho-cosmic sense, this *is* the story. Nancy, a child who had been suicidal since, what? As long as anyone remembered. And Sid, whose fatalism since the breakup of the Sex Pistols had become increasingly obsessive. Every interview the same doomy declarations. And, after all, isn't it the sort of thing a self-destructive rock star would do?

On the face of it Debbie Spungen's story is more convincing than Sid's confession. It fulfills the narrative requirements on a much higher plane, since it includes intent, psychological insight, and romantic closure. Sid and Nancy as a Punk Romeo and Juliet. It's essentially a mythic explanation and, like all myths, true in a way that is truer than any stringing-together of facts could make it.

But, I dunno . . . there's problems with the story. What about the $80?—or maybe it was more than that, say $1,500 or $1,300. Whatever. Even with money taken out to score, it's still a lot of bread, especially in this lowlife scene where people kill each other over a Walkman. Desperation is ugly. And then there's Sid's personality. *Could* he have done it? It's all a little too symmetrical.

The third alternative is a police-procedural type of story and the NYPD homicide squad might have pursued this line of investigation and actually gotten to the bottom of it—maybe not. But after Sid's OD they dropped it. Case closed.

In the third scenario there is a perpetrator other than Sid involved. This hypothetical perp is the Tuinal dealer who was the last person to see Nancy alive. His motive: money, the fifteen hundred bucks. Let's say Nancy caught him. If you, the fly on the wall, could see Nancy going into the bathroom, see her coming out . . .

This is Eliot Kidd talking:

Seeing the guy going through the drawers and catching him taking the money and going after the guy. She would have flipped out if she had caught somebody trying to steal from them. And if this guy had it in him—if you corner a rat, you're going to get bit, you know? I think it's just a shame that when Sid died, they closed the book on Nancy. Somebody got away with murder.

This sounds more like the real story. It has a *real* motive, it has psychology—Sid killing Nancy for any of the above reasons, including his own—seems, on reflection, improbable. He was such a wimp they'd called him Vicious *as a joke.* The Tuinal dealer. The drawer they kept the money in, open, the money missing. Sid filled in the blanks, but what did he know?

Kidd:

I don't think Sid really knew what happened. I mean he wasn't a witness to Nancy dying. What he told me was that he got up, went to the bathroom, and she was lying there dead. The drawer was open where their money was and the money was gone. That's all he knew.

The day after Nancy's death, he hooks up with Michelle Robinson. At his arraignment Sid almost collapses in court. Front page of the *Sun*, October 14, 1978: VICIOUS IN TRANCE. SEX PISTOL IS NEAR COLLAPSE AFTER "I DIDN'T STAB HER" CLAIM. His buddy Jerry Nolan arrives at the court wearing rings made of animal's teeth, a silver skull ring, and brass-studded bracelets. Might as well dress for the occasion, you can never tell who you'll run into at these things.

Back in London, Sex is selling T-shirts at £6.50 each, showing Sid surrounded by dead roses and across the front are the words: I'M ALIVE, SHE'S DEAD, I'M YOURS. It's tasteless and tactless, sublimely tacky and *echt* Punk. Perfectly in character. It's something of a relief that Westwood stuck to her guns, didn't get all mushy and sentimental over this. God knows it was the Punk way to go.

Tabloid headline: NANCY WAS A WITCH! Not only dead, but a dead *witch*. Nancy becomes the butt of sick jokes. They start turning up on the *Tonight Show*. Now this—this is fame! The subject of Johnny's monologue. If only Nancy could have lived to see this! Now all the couples lying in the semi-darkness knew who Nancy Spungen was, knew she was somebody.

On October 23, eleven days after Nancy's death, Sid tries to kill himself with a broken lightbulb. When that fails, he tries to jump out the window at the Seville Hotel. Telling his mum: "I want to die! I want to join Nancy! I didn't keep my part of the bargain!"

Fancy lawyers are hired to defend him, but given the circumstances even the most favorable outcome seals his doom.

Anne Beverley:

She died and he didn't, which made him guilty of manslaughter and, Sorry, here's five years, you'll be out in three. Three years in hard nick in the States? Forget it. He couldn't have done that 'cos he was not a hard man. He was too sweet and soft.

But even this hanging over his head didn't stop his basic nature from acting up. At Hurrah's on December 9, he molests Todd Smith's girlfriend. Todd, Patti Smith's brother, punches him. Sid breaks a beer bottle on the bar and slashes Todd's face. He is cut-up, but not badly. Taken to the emergency ward of Bellevue Hospital, he has some stitches put in and they release him. After the Todd Smith incident, McLaren throws up his hands in exasperation: "He is hellbent on living up to his image."

Since this was a felony and he was out on bail, he is sent to Riker's Island where he gets clean, more or less. His mum smuggles dope into the jail by wearing boots with metal clips on them. When she goes through the metal detector they make her take the boots off, at which point she slips the dope out of the boot and into the cuff of her pants, and since she'd already been searched she gets away with it. Sid comes to the visiting room with his butt greased and sticks it up his ass.

He's released on bail, and then, on Groundhog Day, February 2, 1979, Sid ODs. The evening at Michelle Robinson's (where he was living) started like this.

Eileen Polk:

The English guy had really good dope. They started in the bathroom, and then Sid went in the bathroom. When he came out, he turned all blue and white. We had to take blankets and wrap him up in them. Then he passed out on the bed. It was really kind of scary, and then he woke up and said, "Oh, wow, I'm sorry if I scared you all."

It's getting a little too real. People start to leave. Sid's now in a precarious state because after you've ODed, just falling asleep is enough to kill you. You have to get up, get your blood circulating. A lot of coffee, walk up and down to get the dope out of your system. Because if you don't, you fall asleep again and your body can slow down to the point where the heart fails. But everyone was too out of it. Sid fell back asleep.

Polk:

Anne had to get up early in the morning for a bail bond. She went to the bedroom around seven o'clock, tapped him on the shoulder. He was dead. Michelle lying next to him in the bed.

Maybe he did find that extra packet of dope in his mum's purse and shot some more dope, maybe he took some pills, maybe he just fell asleep. The heroin was very strong.

Daily Mail:

DRUGS KILL PUNK STAR SID VICIOUS.
Punk rock star Sid Vicious, the inadequate youth who turned a tasteful pop gimmick into pathetic real life, died of a heroin overdose yesterday.

Anne Beverley:

He would never have survived. I'm glad he died in view of what happened. Nothing can hurt him anymore. And where could he have gone from where he was at? He couldn't have backed down and done something different like John Lydon has. There was no way he could have reverted and been a pop singer. He was in a corner. The rug was pulled out from under his feet and he would never have survived in an English jail, let alone an American one.

And then, Sid, your record came out and it was a *monster* smash. Okay, it had the train robber Ronnie Biggs—the new lead singer of the Sex Pistols!—singing "A Punk Prayer" on the A-side but we all know it was the B-side that made it a hit—"My Way." More copies, many more copies that either "Holidays" or "God Save the Queen." A bloody fuckin' irony, innit? If that ain't poetic justice and a fitting end to the story of Sid Vicious.

Irony pursued him to the bitter end.

Lydon:

I was utterly appalled when I heard the damned urn with Sid's ashen remains was dropped and smashed to the floor at Heathrow Airport. Classic Sid mythology. Sid was such a hopeless failure at everything, it was so typical, such a horrible way to end—just blowing around the air-conditioning at Heathrow is kind of funny. At least he's occupied. What a marvelous ironic way to end. Poor sod. No peace even for the dead. He was just into chaos for the sheer hell of it and in the end he found it.

Sid was the rock dream emblazoned, the unquestioning zealot, the slightly psychotic fan you'll find any night of the week at the LD50 Lounge, the grungy club where all the rock trolls congregate and *meep-meep-meep* each to each in furious supplication. Look in those eyes! A swirling mass of fused emotion! Beneath the agitated surface are a million Shirley Xs humming like glass bees. Gone to Dimension X. Capable of anything. Ready to undergo whatever it takes to fulfill that mad dream.

> **THERE MIGHT STILL BE A FUTURE FOR ME IN THE WAXWORKS. SAVE ME A PLACE ON THE ETERNITY SHELF. WOULDN'T BE SURPRISED TO FIND MESELF WEDGED IN BETWEEN ARNOLD PALMER AN THOMAS CARLYLE.**

Between the fallen state of the unredeemed fan and the hyperion heights of the star. Sid is stuck in that space between, hovering like an agitated spirit. Never at rest, reeling from one state to the other in perpetual turmoil, haunting his doppelgänger, John Simon Ritchie. He's like some cartoon character, Wile E. Coyote, say, who can't tell the difference between tinsel and TNT and is forever blowing himself to smithereens. He and his hellhound Nancy getting flattened and unrolling themselves. Obsessive idealists in pursuit of the perfect fuckup.